Praises for *Thrive In Five*
Take Charge of Your Finances In Five Minutes a Day

"In the changing credit market, your advice has been in valuable. I have learned what factors make up a credit score and how I can help my clients to improve and avoid hurting their scores."

Rick Bangs, CPA, Richard E. Bangs, Jr CPA 203-252-2100

"Jill is always up-to-date on the latest financial trends and has a stellar way of breaking it down so it's easy to understand. Over the past three years I have followed her newsletter, I have learned how to better and easily manage my finances including budgeting and monitoring my credit report."

ChaChanna Simpson, Owner, Twentity.com

"I have known Jill Russo Foster for several years and her knowledge of personal finances spans many areas such as credit, financing, debt reduction, budgeting and more. She can explain topics in an easy to understand manner so that you know what to do for your situation. Jill has real passion and concern for all she speaks to. She wants people to live better lives by gaining control of their finances."

Marian Cicolello, WBDC, CTWBDC.org

"I have had the pleasure of working with, listening to, and relying on Jill Russo Foster and her deep knowledge of personal finance and credit for the past year. Jill's wealth of experience and "easy to follow" advice is as important to young adults as are the basic educational requirements of Math, English, and Science.

I wholeheartedly recommend Jill's books, seminars, and forums to anyone interested in clean credit, low finance charges, and a bright fiscal future."

>State Representative Fred Camillo, 151st District-CT,
>RepFredCamillo.com

"Jill Russo Foster's book has had a profound effect on how we view our money situation and how we teach our children about finances. I would recommend her books and services to anyone who is serious about saving and responsibly spending their money."

>Michael LaMagna, Esq. 914-534-1048

"This year, far more than any other year, my husband Paul (the neat freak) and I (not so much) have both felt the need to "clean house". In past years we haven't been so aligned on this issue! Thanks to charitable organizations that will come right to your door and pick up unwanted clothing, home furnishings, and assorted tchotchkes and then put them to very good use, it's easier than ever. We've both been feeling weighted down by the unnecessary clutter, and each time we schedule a pickup, it makes us more aware of the things that are not needed, and more eager to schedule another pickup – and more conscious about buying things that aren't truly needed. We've also cut back on buying material gifts for the kids and opting for "experience" gifts such as skiing lessons, tickets to a show, and family outings. Truly, they don't miss the gifts at all – the average toy captures their attention for literally about a week."

Carolyn Aversano, Publisher / Managing Editor, Natural Awakenings Magazine, Fairfield County, ENaturalAwakenings.com

"Thanks to Jill Russo Foster, I balance my checkbook every day. It may sound time-consuming, but it's the easiest thing I've ever done. My husband and I used to overdraw our account because we both use debit cards. Monthly balancing took forever, because we had a hundred tiny transactions and receipts. Jill recommended daily balancing, and that worked for us. I log into our bank account in the morning, balance our transactions, and it only takes a few minutes a day. Thanks, Jill!"

Valerie Crowley, Virtual Assistant, ValerieCrowley.com

"In today's hectic world, it's hard to keep everything in check. Working & raising a family can leave little time for much else. But, our finances are one thing we simply can't let slide. Using her years of experience in the financial world, Jill has made it simple to take charge of your finances, by creating bite-sized pieces that anyone can follow. With something as critical as your finances, you can't afford not to carve out 5 minutes each day to get yourself in gear!"

Kristin Andree, President - Andree Media & Consulting, Author: Don't Make Me Pull This Car Over: A Roadmap for the Working Mom

"Ready to quit worrying and start taking control of your finances? Get a copy of Jill's book (or book title) and get started today!

Jill steps you through different priorities each month, one task a day. Rather than feeling overwhelmed, you'll be amazed at how easy it is to take the things that you have been putting off and finally getting them done!"

**Vicki Heise, Founder, Live Your Healthy Life,
LiveYourHealthyLife.com**

"Finances are a big part of everyday life and can be costly. My client, Jill Russo Foster, breaks down finances into easy to understand steps that will help you get a grasp of your finances."

**Steve Harrison, Bradley Communications, Corp
www.FreePublicity.com**

Thrive In Five
Take Charge of Your Finances In 5 Minutes a Day

by Jill Russo Foster

Thrive In Five
Take Charge of Your Finances In 5 Minutes a Day

© 2011 Money Pit, LLC and Jill Russo Foster

ISBN: 978-0-9817557-2-4

All rights reserved. No part of this publication may be reproduced, stored in a retrieval system, or transmitted in any form or by any means, electronic, mechanical, recording or otherwise, without the prior written permission of the author.

Printed in the USA

Money Pit, LLC
2011

First Edition

DISCLAIMER

This book details the author's personal experiences with and opinions about economical living. The author is not a licensed financial consultant.

The author and publisher are providing this book and its contents on an "as is" basis and make no representations or warranties of any kind with respect to this book or its contents. The author and publisher disclaim all such representations and warranties, including for example warranties of merchantability and financial advice for a particular purpose. In addition, the author and publisher do not represent or warrant that the information accessible via this book is accurate, complete or current.

The statements made about products and services have not been evaluated by the U.S. government. Please consult with your own Certified Public Accountant, Attorney, or Financial Advisor regarding the suggestions and recommendations made in this book.

Except as specifically stated in this book, neither the author or publisher, nor any authors, contributors, or other representatives will be liable for damages arising out of or in connection with the use of this book. This is a comprehensive limitation of liability that applies to all damages of any kind, including (without limitation) compensatory; direct, indirect or consequential damages; loss of data, income or profit; loss of or damage to property and claims of third parties.

You understand that this book is not intended as a substitute for consultation with a licensed financial professional. Before you begin any financial program, or change your lifestyle in any way, you will consult a licensed financial professional to ensure that you are doing what's best for your financial condition.

This book provides content related to topics, finances and economic living. As such, use of this book implies your acceptance of this disclaimer.

Thrive In Five
Take Charge of Your Finances In Five Minutes a Day
is dedicated to my husband Dave for his support and encouragement throughout this book and many other wonderful people, without whom this book wouldn't have been possible.

My thanks to the many colleagues and friends, who have stood by me with unwavering support and encouragement to write this book. Thank you to Bill Heise, Patricia Maher and Lori Poniatowski for helping me put this together. Thank you to my Sacred Circle Mastermind group for your ongoing support, feedback and opinions; to Valerie Crowley, the best Virtual Assistant anyone could ever want; to Vicki Heise who's daily calls mean so much to me; photographer Regina Madwed and the people at BookLocker for their expertise. Lastly, to all the people who are too numerous to name individually, who are there for me,
I am truly grateful for you.

Thank you to all

Table of Contents

Introduction – My Story 1
January – Analyzing Your Bills 5
February – Reduce or Eliminate Expenses 20
March – Saving More 33
April - Organization 46
May – Clutter Cleaning 55
June – Selling or Donating 66
July – Credit 76
August – Debt Reduction 96
September – No Spending Month 107
October – More Income / Planning Ahead 116
November – The Holidays 127
December – Money Drains 138
Appendix 149
Resources 161
Books 168

FOREWARD

My hope is that you read this book and follow the tips that appeal to you. You don't need to do each and every step. Work on what's important to you, at this point in your life. This book is not meant to be a burden. It's to improve your finances. Everyone starts from where they are. There is no shame, guilt or blame for what has happened to you in the past.

Today is the start of the next phase of your financial life. Starting today, you will make informed choices that are right for you. Just paying attention to your finances and making conscious choices will improve your financial picture. Good money habits begin with new information that leads to better choices.

Ask yourself, "What is the one thing you need to know now to improve your finances?" Take a moment to come up with the answer. That is what you should focus on first. Good luck on your journey to improve your financial situation.

INTRODUCTION – MY STORY

I was born and raised in Fairfield County, Connecticut. My father was a hard working man who worked two jobs as far back as I can remember. My mother was a bookkeeper and handled the all family finances. We were a very close family who lived a modest lifestyle with occasional splurges on education, food, clothing and vacations.

When I should have been learning about money in my teens, my mother was diagnosed with a terminal illness. My first job after college, I entered the working world and started my banking career. I began my career in a very affluent area with clients that were celebrities, professional athletes etc. I watched how they lived. They drove the cars I wanted and wore the most beautiful designer clothes, but they were also on the overdraft list every day. You can imagine me being tempted by all of this because I had no financial guidance.

When my mother passed away, I inherited some money which I foolishly went through living the lifestyle I thought I wanted. And when that money ran out, I got credit cards and continued that same lifestyle, until I maxed out 27 credit cards. Then life as I knew it had to change.

I was in my 20's, so you know I didn't want to be home every night or not wear the latest fashion. I was in the financial field, so bankruptcy wasn't an option. I would lose my job and career if my credit suffered, so I had to make some radical changes. I got a part time job and an occasional third job to be able to pay more than the minimum on this debt. Eventually years later, I got it all paid off.

Then I chose to work for myself. With self employment came many more financial challenges. How do you stick to your financial plan when there is no money coming in this month or when clients are not paying you on a timely basis? I chose to close that business and started my mortgage company, The Mortgage Arrangers, LLC where money collection was not going to be an issue. I still had the peaks and valleys of cash flow depending on how the home buying market was going. Some months I had extra money while others were a bit short, which was a challenge, but at least when a mortgage closed I knew I was going to get paid.

I needed a plan to live by and I had to figure out what was important to me. I needed to learn how I could have what I wanted and still have fun while still living within my means. So that became my mission. I have made many mistakes but fortunately I have learned from all of them. To this day, my husband and I still do many things that are low cost like going to movies in the park, using the services of the public library and having pot luck dinners with friends. We choose to live frugally, but we do have planned splurges so that we don't feel deprived.

As you can see, just like most people, I have had (and continue to have) issues with debt, not saving as much as I want, keeping my emergency savings built up and dealing with things I want but probably don't really need. My goal for this book is to share with you what I have learned and how I deal with the everyday problems of managing my finances.

I personally use many of the tips in this book. My January ritual is to see where my husband and I are financially and to reassess our bills. I am always looking for more ways to save money.

My credit report has always been (and will continue to be) important to me. Just like you I am tempted by sales and discounted items. I have to take time to decide if something is really a bargain and if I really need it. Just because something is a great buy, doesn't mean you should buy it. I have to continuously remind myself of this.

As you work through this book, I would love to know what you found most helpful.

Please send your comments to Book@JillRussoFoster.com . I look forward to hearing from you.

Jill Russo Foster
Money Pit, LLC
www.JillRussoFoster.com

January – Analyzing Your Bills

It's January, the start of a new year. For most people, it's the time when you start to receive your holiday bills and are amazed at what you spent. You vow to never do this again. But isn't that what you said last year and the year before? This year will be different!

By this time next year you will be in charge of your finances with a new thought process that will lead to good money habits.

Since January is a financial month of bills and the start of getting your finances in order for tax season, I am going to start with your bills. You are going to look at each and every bill to see where you can make changes.

1 Holiday
Since today is a holiday, I am going to give you a one day break. But if you want to get a jump on tomorrow, go ahead.

2 Gathering
Today is a day of gathering. I want you to get out your bills. Gather your utilities (electric, gas, oil, water, telephone, cell phone), mortgage(s), insurance (car, home / renters, umbrella) and any others. You are going to tackle one bill a day over the next several days.

3 Electric Bill

Take a good look at your electric bill and the charges. Can you reduce your monthly electric expense? You know the money saving things you are supposed to be doing – shutting the lights when you're not in the room, changing to CFL light bulbs, unplugging things that are energy hogs (when you're not using them) etc. Hopefully you are doing this already - if not, start to. It will save you money!

If you are in a state that has deregulated electricity, check out what other electric providers companies are offering. I switched last year and I am saving approximately 17% each month. That's a savings of $204 a year on a current bill of $100 a month. There is no difference that I can tell with the service. Still one bill to pay each month and one company to call for a power outage. Today, I want you to check with your specific state to see if it offers deregulated electricity. If they do, then look into your options today.

4 Gas Bill

Can you do the same with your gas bill? For me, I have a gas stove and that is all. If you heat by gas, this could be a big expense for you. Do you have a programmable thermostat to keep the heat lower when you are out of the home? Can you lower the temperature a few degrees when you are home? All these things add up.

If you heat your home with natural gas, then depending on the price of gas you may want to talk to your provider about locking in a rate. This can be a dilemma – you love it if you lock and prices go up but get annoyed if you lock and prices go down. If locking is available, ask questions before you make your choice. What can you do today to lower your bill?

5 Oil Bill

This is a big one for me. I currently live in a home heated by oil. A few years ago, I made the mistake of not locking in and the price of oil went up substantially. I have learned my lesson, but it's not what you are thinking – I haven't locked my oil rate. I phoned several companies to see what they were offering for new customers and I switched companies. I found a company that offered a 40¢ per gallon savings for paying the bill the day the oil was delivered. I have to pay the bill anyway, so it didn't matter to me. By paying the driver if I am going to be there or at the office if I am not it saves me postage too.

Make time to call other oil companies to see what they are offering. If you find a better option, call your current company to see if they will match and or beat that option. It's up to you to do the calling to save the money here.

6 Water Bill

You've heard about all the tips about using less water – low flow faucets, shorter showers, etc. I'm not sure there is much else you can do to lower your water bill except for using less water but there is a big one. Check for leaks, drips and running toilets. I have a friend who couldn't figure out why the bill was so high – until she discovered the running toilet. She spent a few dollars for a plumber and reduced her monthly bill by $30.

For those of you who are environmentally conscious, what I did this year was invest in a rain barrel. I purchased this big rain barrel. I am not handy so I didn't install it with my gutters; I just took the lid off the top and put screen material around the opening. I don't want to breed mosquitoes. I use this water for my flowers, the vegetable garden and to water my inside plants. This summer I received my lowest water bill to date since moving in to the home. Summer is usually my highest water bill. Consider buying a rain barrel and make some other changes to lessen your water consumption.

7 Telephone Bill

Do you have a home phone? If you answered no, you get a day off. If you answered yes, are you with the best company with the right plan for your needs? Consider what your needs are and investigate your options. Is there money you are wasting by being on the wrong plan? A few calls a month, maybe you should be on an economy plan. Live on the phone, there are plans for that too. Determine what your needs are and get on that plan. Maybe you can eliminate this cost all together if you don't need that home number.

If you have internet service at home, consider using an alternative telephone service for your long distance calls. These services can cut your phone bill substantially or possibly make it free.

8 Cell Phone Bill

Yesterday, I spoke about home phones, today let's talk about cell phones. Are you on the right plan for your needs? Do you currently have unused minutes that you are paying for? I know that I eliminated some features from my bill and lowered my monthly minute allowance for a savings of about $20 a month. Can you do the same?

Talk to your provider about what you can eliminate. Make sure you understand what the potential costs could be before making any changes. Are there penalties for switching mid-contract? Does this start your agreement again? Know the consequences and consider them before you make a move. You may be better off waiting until your agreement comes up for renewal. Investigate the details and make an informed choice.

9 Catch Up Day

This is your day to look at another bill that I didn't mention. Or you might have been too busy to complete one of the suggestions. Today is a catch up day.

10 Mortgage Bill

If you are like most people, your house (and the resulting mortgage) is the biggest purchase you will ever make in your lifetime. Making sure you pay your mortgage on time and avoid the late fee is your biggest savings. If you pay extra principle with your mortgage payment you will be paying your mortgage faster. The faster you pay your mortgage, the less interest you will pay. Aren't you looking forward to the day when your mortgage is paid in fill?

Develop a plan to pay extra on your mortgage. You don't have to pay extra each month, even every other month will pay it off faster and save you interest. If you are not sure how you can afford to pay extra right now, don't worry. When you get to future chapters, I will be suggesting ways to increase your income and find more money.

11 Private Mortgage Insurance

Most people don't know if they have this or not. Did you put a 20% down payment on your home when you purchased it? If you didn't and you have a first mortgage that was more than 80%, of the purchase price, you have private mortgage insurance. Check out your bill carefully to see your payment breakdown. When you believe that you have more than 20% equity in your home (not including your second mortgage / home equity line (or loan), you will need to contact your lender. They will tell you the steps to have this cost removed from your monthly bill. This can save you a substantial amount each and every month. Make a call to your lender today to see if you have private mortgage insurance.

If you have private mortgage insurance but don't have the 20% equity yet, then keep this in mind for the future. Your lender will not tell you when you should request this nor will this drop off automatically. This is up to you to keep track of.

12 Car Insurance Bill

This is a big project, so I am giving you multiple days. First call your company or agent to see if you have the proper coverage for your situation. Discuss what items you might want to eliminate that are unnecessary. You may want to raise you deductible. Only do this to an amount that you know you can come up with if you need to. We will talk about your savings in a later month. Today, make sure you have the proper coverage for your situation.

13 Car Insurance Bill

If you have an independent insurance agent, you may want to ask them to do this for you. Otherwise, do this on your own. Contact other insurance companies to get estimates based on what coverage you need. Remember that you need to be with an insurance company that has a good rating.

A few years back, I made the switch from one company to another company. There were three policies – car, home and umbrella – and the total savings was just less than $1,000 per year with the same coverage. This was a no brainer to switch. Periodically, I do call and check the competitions rates.

Remember, the more policies you have with one company the lower you rates will be because of multi-policy discounts. Also remember that just because the company you started out with was the best price then, it may not still be the cheapest.

14 Roadside Assistance

I analyzed our car insurance as well as other related bills and added coverage to my insurance. For example, I added roadside assistance for less than $20 per year for two cars and was able to eliminate the auto club bill that was over $100 per year. The concession is that I have to pay for towing and then submit a bill for reimbursement. This was a no brainer for me saving 80%. What do you need to change?

15 Insurance Deductibles

What is the deductible on your insurance policies? Do you keep it low to have less out of pocket money if a claim arises? Do you keep the deductible high and pay less each year on the premium?

My suggestion is to keep it high, especially on your car insurance. With most companies offering a lower deductible with every so many months you have no accident, that high deductible will be lower without the higher premium.

Today, look at your finances and figure out what dollar amount you could afford to come up with in a hurry and then consider raising your deductible.

16 Renter Insurance

If you are a renter, you're probably thinking why do I need insurance? The answer is that your landlords insurance doesn't cover your personal property – TV and electronics, clothing etc. Nor does it cover things that you are personally liable for (your negligence). If you are a renter, I strongly encourage you to get this insurance. This is so inexpensive and will be a big benefit to you if you need it.

I know of many people who have had a loss of their personal stuff through no fault of their own. For a small amount of money, you could be covered versus having a big expense of replacing the damaged items.

17 Umbrella Insurance

Some of you have probably never heard of an umbrella insurance policy. This too is another low cost insurance that can save you money if you need it. Umbrella insurance covers you above your limits of your other policies. It gives you additional coverage in case you need it. This is something that gives me peace of mind for a minimal cost. Just one accident and you could be sued for thousands of dollars. Check with your insurance agent or company today and discuss this policy and the benefits.

18 Catch Up Day

This is a busy month and I don't want you to fall behind. Use today to catch up on anything that you haven't done or need more time to do. If you have done everything then take the day off or read ahead.

19 Other Bills

Do you have other bills that I haven't mentioned that you want to take the time to go over? Now is the time to look over those bills to see if you can reduce or eliminate them.

20 Bank Accounts

Are your bank accounts insured by the FDIC (Federal Deposit Insurance Company) or by a credit union's NCSIF (National Credit Share Insurance Fund)? Make sure your accounts are protected by contacting your bank / credit union. If your accounts are NOT protected, move them to an institution that is today.

If your accounts are protected, then are you below the deposit limit? Generally, you should not have more than $250,000 in one bank. This is per bank, not per branch. If you have more than $250,000 total in that bank, move some of your money to another bank or credit union.

21 Bank Accounts

Are you with the right bank for you? The best solution would be to get the highest interest rate on your accounts (this includes your checking) and pay nothing in fees. Does this sound like you account?

If not, take the time to explore what your bank offers. Maybe you are in the wrong type of account. You can either do this with a website search, a phone call or stopping by the branch. Today is the day to research your bank. With bank fees being limited with the new Credit Card Act, banks are changing and adding fees to make up for the lost income.

Local banks and credit unions rather than the big national banks are usually a good place to look for low cost accounts.

22 Banking

Are you all set with your bank and accounts? If not, today is the day to do research on other banks and credit unions and see what they have to offer.

If you are thinking about changing, you need to consider these questions
    Will you bank accounts be insured?
    Are the locations convenient to your life?
    Do they have ATM's that are where your life takes you?

If the answer to any of these questions is "no", then move on and look somewhere else.

Other questions that you should ask -
> What is the interest rate I am receiving?
> What fees will I have to pay?
> What are the other fees associated with the account?

23 Reconciling Your Account

I can't say this enough, but you do need to balance you accounts at least monthly. Whether you do this the manual way with a bank statement or with software, you need to know how much money you have available at all times.

With the new banking rules about not letting you overdrawing your account, this is more important than ever. It's a total waste of money to pay the bank unnecessary fees such as overdraft or uncollected funds. From today on, vow to keep great records so you save this money.

If you haven't done this in a really long time, balance your account today. For those of you who keep good records, I suggest that you monitor your accounts weekly to keep an eye on what going on. You can never monitor too much.

24 Catch Up Day

This is a busy month and I don't want you to fall behind. Use today to catch up on anything that you haven't done or need more time to do. If you've done everything, then take the day off or read ahead.

25 Annual Payments

Some bills give you the option of paying an annual payment or splitting your payment into multiple payments (quarterly, monthly etc). If you take a monthly payment and multiply it by 12, you will find that you are paying more than the annual payment. It's a service charge to not pay your bill in full. Why not be proactive and save your money so that you can make your payment in full annually and save that service charge.

I know for me, I plan these so that they don't all come in one month. They are spread out over the year. The year starts with timeshare maintenance in January, car and umbrella insurance comes in February; April is long term care and December is life insurance. All are paid in one payment to save the additional fees.

26 Add On Fees

Add on fees can be a big money drain. It needs to stop here. This can be a big issue for many. What I am talking about is those fees that you owe because you are not on top of your finances, including the fee for paying a bill late, the fee for a returned check or paying your bill the day it's due and having to pay a fee to expedite the payment. If this sounds like you, then vow to stop that right now.

Today is the day to set up your bill paying system, so that you will be on top of your finances. Think about your habits and then pick a spot to set up everything. This is what I personally do and it works great for me. I have a rack on the kitchen wall that has three sections. The bottom section is for bills that have to be paid. When I open the mail, they are immediately put there. The middle section is for bank receipts, that includes the actual bank receipts for deposits and ATM transactions and all the debit card charges too. When the bank statement comes, I have everything I need in one place and can balance my checkbook easily. The top section is for credit card receipts. When my credit card statement comes, I can compare the receipts to the statement and check all the transactions.

Find a place and a system that works for you today. Make it work for you, so that you will use it from today forward. If you are on top of your finances, then you will not have to pay any of those add on fees.

27 Payment Reminders

Still need more help? Then set up payment reminders to remind you when a bill is due.

Did you know that it's your responsibility to make a payment even if you didn't receive the bill in the mail? Most online banking websites offer this reminder service for your online bill payments. If you don't use online bill pay, you can set up a reminder in your calendar (paper, computer, cell phone etc). Whatever you use, there is a way to do this. Figure out what will work for you and set it up.

28 Unseen Bills

These are those bills that you don't get in the mail. Those things that you are set up to automatically renew. The service will tell you that they take the hassle out of remembering to pay by setting automatic payments up for you. Yes, they do take the hassle out of it for you. But, the other side is that you might not remember this bill and therefore don't look at it to cancel it or to shop around for a cheaper service. Examples of this can be subscriptions and memberships. Today, think about what you have in your life that happens automatically. Is it that gym membership that you bought last January that you don't use? Is it the magazine subscription that renews automatically and is billed to your credit card? What's happening automatically in your life?

29 Energy Audits

One of the greatest things I had done to my home this year was an energy audit. There were several great aspects to this. The fee was nominal (less than $50) and our electric company offered this to its customers as an insert in their bill. The company came and did the energy audit and told me about all the energy leaks. Then, they went through my home and made the small repairs – replaced any light bulbs with CFL's (I had no idea that you could have CFL light bulbs with dimmers), caulked any air leaks, replaced the shower and sink faucets with low flow versions, put door sweeps on the doors to stop drafts, insulated the water pipes and more. All this was included in my nominal fee. I think I got my money's worth. Check with your state or utility providers to see what they are offering you.

30 Catch Up Day

Did you do everything I suggested this month? Is there anything that you want to do with your bills that I didn't mention? Do you need more time to complete anything? Today and tomorrow are the days to do this. If you done everything then take the day(s) off or read ahead.

31 Catch Up Day

This is a catch up day to finish anything you haven't completed.

Notes – use this space for any follow up to schedule, thoughts and ideas for yourself

February – Reduce or Eliminate Expenses

Now that you have gone over your bills and you see how much money you are spending, how can you reduce or eliminate some of your expenses? In my experience it is not the big items that cause the leaks in the budget, it's the small drips that add up. Here are some of my suggestions to save you money. Some suggestions are going to make sense to you and others won't. Do what makes sense to you and skip the ones that don't. As you reread this book, you might try others.

1 Use Cash

Use cash - sounds simple enough, but can you do this? When I say cash I mean the actual bills and coins, not a debit card. Using cash for your purchases makes you have to think about what you are purchasing, the cost and how much money you have with you. You can't spend more than you have with you!

Try this – what have you go to lose? It really stops the impulse shopping and makes you think about your purchase. In addition, I personally find that if I have large bills in my wallet, I am less likely to break a $50 or $100 to make a purchase than if I am carrying smaller bills.

2 Subscriptions

If you are like my household, we had magazine subscriptions coming in weekly, monthly etc. We didn't seem to have the time to read as many as we were getting. So they piled up. Does this sound familiar?

I personally didn't renew any of my subscriptions. I was hesitant at first, but really haven't missed them. Most of the time, I can read the article I am interested in online without paying for it. A couple of times a year, I will buy one of the magazines to read. Cutting out just one subscription saved me $28 / year. See how much you can save.

If you really can't give a subscription up, you can try what my husband did. He split the cost of a subscription with a friend. You are getting the magazine at half the cost and saving paper too. Think outside the box for how you can save.

3 Cell Phone Insurance

When a friend of mine talked about cell phone insurance and how much it cost her, I told her what I do. I have never purchased cell phone insurance. I keep the old phone and accessories in a drawer after getting the new phone. If something were to happen to my phone, I could then active my old phone versus buying a new one (usually at the full price).

Cell phone insurance seems to run between $5 and $10 per month, for a total of $60 to $120 per year. Typically you have a two year contract, so double that amount. Add in the deductible and you have paid much more than the cost of the phone (if you actually need it). Do the math before you purchase this insurance.

4 Lower Your Car Insurance

Did you know that you can lower your car insurance by taking a safe driving class? I took a safe driving class and was able to lower my car insurance premium. For me, I took eight hours of classroom time (that's the Connecticut requirement for the class) at a cost of $16 and was able to save $100 per year for the next three years. I even learned a thing or two. Check with your insurance company to see how much you can save, then schedule a class near you.

5 Repair Versus Replace

We all know that things breakdown. Typically we toss them out and purchase a new one. Consider repairing an item before getting rid of it. We had a problem with our ice maker, it wasn't making ice. Before calling the repair man, my husband read the troubleshooting section of the manual and checked online. He was able to figure the problem out. That saved us the cost of a service call. We had a power washer that wouldn't start after the winter months. A trip to the service shop for about $100 for the repair was more cost effective than buying a new machine.

If you need to have something repaired, you need to determine what a new item will cost you. Then you can make a determination as to how much is worth spending on a repair. You might be surprised at how much you save.

6 Catch Up Day

This is a busy month and I don't want you to fall behind. Use today to catch up on anything that you haven't done or need more time to do. If you've done everything, then take the day off or read ahead.

7 Extended Warranties

In my opinion, these are not a good use of your money. Most major purchases come with a warranty to start at no cost to you. Rarely does a product need repair immediately, but you are covered if it does. After that period, you will be paying a fee if something goes wrong.

I have a friend who pays for a service contract for his appliances. Recently, his washer wasn't fixable, so he was given a substantial amount of money as a credit towards a new washer. Sounds great doesn't it? Let's examine this. He paid a fee every year for the past 35 years for an extended warranty. I don't know how much he paid, but let's say $50 per year for 35 years is $1,750 to get about $700 off a new washer. I can't say how many service calls he used in the 35 years, but I'm guessing he would have been better off saving the $50 and buying the washer with cash. Think about what it costs for the typical repairs (if you can't do them yourselves) versus what you would pay for the service call.

I have to admit that I just replaced my shredder and did buy the extended warranty on this item. It was $8 for a two year warranty and I thought this was a good buy, since the shredder costs $100 + to purchase. I use a shredder constantly and seem to go through them within the two years. Think before you make a purchase to see if it's cost effective for you.

8 Storage Space

I'm sure you can guess my opinion on this. Paying for storage for stuff that you don't have room for is a big waste of money. There are only a few exceptions – storing your stuff while your home is being renovated, if you are in between homes for a short period of time etc. Getting rid of or selling the stuff, not only eliminates the store space fees but could also put money in your pocket. What do you use your storage space for? Is it time to get rid of the stuff?

9 Dental Work

Do you avoid going to the dentist because of the cost? Have you ever thought about having your dental cleaning done at a college? Some dental colleges offer people a substantial savings to have your dental work done by a student. Check out your closest dental school to see what they have to offer. Having a low cost cleaning may prevent major problems later.

10 Prescriptions

Prescriptions, even with an insurance plan can be a budget buster for many. Make sure you ask your doctor or pharmacist about generic prescriptions. Check out other pharmacies, drug prices tend to differ. Check out your local supermarket pharmacy for prescriptions. I know that my supermarket offers certain FREE antibiotics.

My 90 day prescription at Costco is less expensive than using the mail order pharmacy that is associated with my medical insurance. Costco is 30% less than my co-pay. Every few bucks count. Check around to see how you can save money.

11 Paper Checks

Do you use paper checks anymore? For certain tax related expenses, I do. If you use checks, don't order them from your bank unless you get FREE checks. Buying checks from your bank can cost you 50% more than buying them yourself.

12 Online Bill Pay

This is a service that most people either use and couldn't live without it or are completely against. I do pay my bills online and that eliminates the cost of postage – no more stamps. It's easy to set up. You can pay your bills in advance, so that you won't miss a due date when you are away or unavailable to make the payment. You can set up automatic bill pay for each and every month if the bill amount stays the same, or you can have email reminders to tell you that a bill is due.

There are a few things that I want to caution you about online bill pay. First, you should always initiate your transaction from your banks website. You have more control over the transaction in case something goes wrong. If you do this from the creditor's website and there is a problem, you could be left with no protection. In addition, if you do the payment from each creditor's website, each will have your banking information. This puts your personal information in the hands of many more people. More people having this information can lead to the possibility of identity theft. The less people and companies that have your information, the better off it is for you.

13 Price Protection
This has happened to all of us. You go out and you buy something and then you notice that next week the item goes on sale. Did you know that most stores will give you the difference back? Each store has its own policy for the time, but typically if the item goes on sale within a 14 day period, you can get the difference back.

14 Price Matching
Some stores will honor other stores' prices or coupons. You will not know unless you ask. What is the worst that will happen? The store will say "no". Then you have to make a choice. Keep this in mind as you shop for items that you need.

Before you go shopping for an item, check online and in your local paper, etc for the best price in your area. If the lowest price is at a store that is not convenient for you, talk with the manager in the store that is and show them your research. Some stores will match their competitors' pricing.

15 Discounts
Are you a member of certain organizations such as AAA or AARP? These and others offer you discounts on a wide variety of products. We have purchased an Entertainment Book for the area we are going to for their numerous discounts on everything from restaurants to stores. Check out their websites for the list of discounts that might be of interest to you.

Before planning a vacation, we have searched and used discounts for hotels, rental cars and attractions. Our AAA office offers reduced price movie tickets that you purchase from them.

16 Reward Points

These days almost every credit card or membership I have offers rewards points for discounted or free items. I am talking about all the benefits that come from your daily life, airline miles, hotel frequent stay programs, credit card benefits, gift cards etc

I use these services frequently. One credit card offers points for everything I charge. I use these points to purchase gift cards for when I need one. Even my electric company offers points towards merchandise, discounted tickets etc. I use hotel points for free nights. Being a member of some of these programs gives you extra benefits.

I was attending a conference out of state and went a few days early. I used my points for the first night of the hotel stay. When I arrived they upgraded me to a suite as a loyal member of the hotel chain. It was a nice treat! I personally have not had trouble using my airline miles for free flights or upgrades. It's taken some thought and coordination, but I have flown to Alaska and Hawaii in recent years using free miles.

Not every program is right for you. Look over the details and make an informed choice. Yes, it does take some thought but that effort can benefit you in savings.

17 Catch Up Day

This is a busy month and I don't want you to fall behind. Use today to catch up on anything that you haven't done or need more time to do. If you've done everything, then take the day off or read ahead.

18 Coupons

This is a love it or hate it subject. People who use coupons swear by them, while others are very much against them. Which are you?

I think I personally fall somewhere in the middle. I will never be one of those people you read about who buys $100 of groceries for $20 with coupons. I frankly don't have the time or want to exert the effort to do coupons to that extent. But I do use them. If they are mailed to me, I will save the ones that I might use. I will go through the Sunday newspaper for the coupons.

Here is the but – I don't buy an item because I have a coupon for it. So if there is a coupon for something I use and I need to purchase it, then that is fine. I will try to combine my shopping list of what's on sale with a coupon. For me, some weeks I save a few dollars and other weeks I can save $20. I have a balance in my life of what efforts I am willing to make in exchange for the return.

Tip – if you are getting your coupons from the internet, create a separate email account for all these emails. You can look at them at your leisure or when you have a need and not clog up your regular email account.

19 Borrowing / Sharing

Can you borrow something versus buying it? When I started my first company I shared space with a friend who was starting his company. To save money, we each bought one piece of office equipment. I bought the fax and he bought the copier. So when I needed to copy something, I would use his copier and when he needed to fax something he would use mine. A little creative thinking saved us money. What can you borrow versus buy? Your local library is a great place to start.

20 Swap or Trade

What do you want to swap or trade? If it is books, DVDs, movies, video games and you want to do this on the internet, there are a couple of websites that specialize in this, www.Swap.com and www.Half.com. Check them out and see if they are right for you.

You can also look around in your community. Mothers have been doing this for years – swapping children's clothing their child has outgrown with another mother. Think of other ways and people who might benefit from this.

If you can have something you need or want and can get it for less, why wouldn't you do this? Buying or swapping items are a big money saver and can help anyone's budget.

21 Energy Hogs

Did you know that some electronics in your home use energy even when they are turned off? Yes, it's true. Unplug or turn off the power strip when your electronics are not in use. Especially, if you are going to be away from home for a prolonged period. You will see a difference in your electric bill.

22 Energy Efficiency

We all know we should do these things, but do you? Change your light bulbs to energy efficient ones, lower your heat thermostat or raise your air conditioning thermostat when no one is home, use low flow faucets and shower heads.

There is a kilowatt meter that you can use to tell if your appliance is running efficiently. Follow the instructions to see if your appliance is using too much energy. It may be time to replace it.

23 Appliances

Before you replace that appliance, do your research. Save time and check out www.ApplianceRebate.com. This website will search by your location for rebates from manufacturers, utility companies and more to inform you about what is available and even give you the forms necessary for the rebate.

24 Still Too Much Money Going Out?

If you think you can save more and want to try, go to www.BillShrink.com. The website offers you better pricing for what you want. For example, enter your cell phone information about your current plan and answer a few questions and Bill Shrink will give you a recommendation.

Tip – since most of these websites will ask you for an email address, you may want to set up a new account so you are not receiving numerous emails in your regular address. Or you can do this cost comparison on your own with a few phone calls or website searches.

25 Coffee

This can add up to a big expense if you buy it at a coffee shop or store every day. Make extra coffee (or whatever your choice of drink is) at home to bring with you. Have a coffee pot at your office. My husband did this for years. He programmed the coffee maker to have it ready for when he arrived.

26 Lunch

I almost always bring my lunch or snacks with me. Not only does this save money, I make healthier choices. All it takes is a little planning ahead. I make more dinner than we will eat so that there are leftovers. Then, all I have to do is assemble what I am taking in the morning. If I know that I have a busy week and can't cook more the night before, I cook extra on the weekend. Think and plan ahead.

27 Meal Planning

Cooking ahead for those busy times will save you money. Make a double portion of a meal to freeze for another night. When you know your schedule is going to make dinner difficult, take out a meal in the morning to defrost for when you get home. This will save you the cost of takeout food.

28 Habits

What's your money habit that is costing you? You know what I mean. Can you give up just one habit? I am not asking you to give up your life. Try giving up one habit for a week and see how you feel. Can you continue doing without it? You can always go back to it if you find you just can't live without it.

Check out some of the books in the resource section. Some of the suggestions are things that I easily incorporated into my life.

Notes – use this space for any follow up to schedule, thoughts and ideas for yourself

March – Saving More

In March I am asking you to think outside the box and push your saving even higher. First, you need to know what money is coming in and what is going out. I am going to give you a week to work on this project.

Then I am going to suggest things to you that you might not want to do – then don't. Other things might intrigue you, try them. Each effort you make will save you money. Try something now and when you reread the book, try others.

1 Knowing Where You Stand

To take charge of your finances you have to know where you stand. I know that some people will want to shut the book at this point, but don't. It's not going to be that hard for you to do this. This is not a one day project, so don't panic. You have a week to do this for yourself. No one is going to look at this, but you will need this as a starting point. Take the time to do this.

Start with my budget or spending plan worksheet in the appendix section. As you are preparing for your taxes, you will have this information readily available. For your income, look at your W-2 forms and divide by 12 for the income. This will give you a monthly figure. If you have 1099's then you can do the same. Or take you pay stub and multiply by the number of pay periods in the year. Remember to add any other income – pensions, rental income, investments etc to get a clear picture.

2 Knowing Where You Stand

Today, continue with your income section. Make sure you have everything you can think of. Use my sample form in the appendix to jog your memory.

3 Knowing Where You Stand

Now, let's look at your fixed expenses – mortgage or rent, insurance premiums (home, auto, health, disability, long term etc), utilities (if possible, take an average of the last year), and any other fixed recurring payments that apply to your situation.

4 Knowing Where You Stand

Continue with yesterday's fixed expenses.

5 Knowing Where You Stand

Now for those variable expenses – groceries, eating out, entertainment, gifts, travel etc. I find this the hardest category to come up with a number. The easiest way is to check your bank and credit card statements for the costs to come up with a number. Try looking at three to six months and taking an average to see what you "normally" spend on these kinds of expenses.

6 Knowing Where You Stand

Continue with yesterday's variable expenses. Don't forget to include the things that are paid for in cash – tips, babysitting, coffee, newspapers, lottery (you get the idea).

7 Knowing Where You Stand

Now comes the day to add up your numbers to see where you stand. Which side is bigger? Is there more money coming in than going out? Or is it the other way around? That is all I am asking you to figure out here.

You need to determine what the next step is for you. If you are like most people, you will need to get your expenses down or generate more income. Don't panic! In the coming months, I will discuss raising your income and reducing your debt. You may want to go back to February to review the "Reduce or Eliminate Expenses" chapter again.

For the rest of this month, I will talk about ways to save more. Again, these are suggestions that you can chose to do or not. Only implement ways that seem right to you now. Then go back at a later date and try others.

8 Catch Up Day

This was a big project to give you to do in five minutes a day for seven days. I am giving you two additional days to wrap up this snapshot of where you stand.

9 Catch Up Day

Continue to finish this step.

10 Save Your Change

I never use change when making a purchase. I always get coins back. At the end of the day, that change goes into a bank in my home. At the end of the month, I bring it to the bank (mine has a free coin counting machine) and deposit it to my savings account. I average about $20 per month. You might be thinking what's $20, but for me, $240 a year is a car payment. Learn to think with the bigger number and it will feel worthwhile to you.

11 Rebates

Will you do the paperwork? Each year I purchase my antivirus software just after Thanksgiving. Not only is it on sale, but I usually get a three user pack for less than $10 with the rebates. I make sure to do the paperwork the day of purchase while I still have everything I need. When the rebate comes, it's like FREE money.

12 Web Shopping

Do you shop on the web? Do you just go to a particular website and make a purchase? You might want to think about price shopping for the lowest price. I know that this can take up your precious time. The website www.Billeo.com offers to search as a browser to notify you of discount coupons that are available.

13 Gardening

I was brought up with a family that had a backyard garden. Especially now when I am making a great effort to eat more fresh and locally grown food, the garden makes sense. The garden my grandparents had when I was growing up took most of the backyard. Unfortunately, that doesn't work for me. I have to keep mine small so that it's something that I can manage and is not too overwhelming for me. I start about this time of year with seeds inside to start my plants (although in some years I buy plants in another month).

You can do this too. You can have a garden in your backyard or a container on your deck – whatever works for your situation. You can grow whatever appeals to you, from herbs to tomatoes. There is nothing better than going out and picking what you want to eat when you are ready to eat it.

You are probably thinking what does this have to do with saving money – lots! The more you grow the less money you spend at the grocery store. Lettuce is a very easy vegetable to grow. Put seeds in the soil and within two weeks you have lettuce for your salads. No more buying lettuce at the grocery store or wanting a salad only to find out that the lettuce in your fridge is bad. You pick the lettuce leaves as you need them. Think about what you would like to grow today.

14 Time With Friends

Do you ever want to spend time with friends, but don't want to spend lots of money on a restaurant? I know that I really want to spend time with people. Consider a potluck dinner.

You can select the house (yours or theirs) and then everyone brings something. To kick it up a notch, try having a menu based on a certain cuisine. I and some friends got together at a friend's home and the theme was Chinese food. The hostess made moo shoo pork and the rest of us brought the sides.

I know people who get together on a regular basis for dinner clubs, wine tastings, movie nights and more. What appeals to you? Think about whom you could plan this with for a fun night. Make plan with your friends.

15 Alternate Suggestions
Want to spend time with a friend at no cost? Try going for a walk and having a chat with your friend. Save the cost of food and get your exercise in. This is a fun thing to do and has many health benefits.

16 Dinner with a Twist
If you want something more than pot luck but don't' want to pay a fortune for dinner out try a BYOB restaurant. Check around, some restaurants will let you bring you own bottle of wine instead of purchasing a bottle from them. Ask because there could be a corkage fee for bringing your own bottle. Usually your favorite bottle of wine can be double the price of what you would pay for it retail. Check with your state, because some states will let you bring the partial bottle home and others won't. This is a way of having dinner out and still saving some money if you are a wine drinker.

17 Movie Night At Home
How about a movie marathon at home? Go to your local library and borrow several movies and then have popcorn and beverages in front of your TV. Or if the library doesn't have what you want, you could rent them at your local grocery store movie kiosk for a minimal cost. If you are a Netflix member, that will work if you have a compatible game console.

Think about ways you can have fun with minimal or no money. Make your list today and then plan those times into your calendar and invite friends to join you if you want.

18 Games Night

Last year while visiting friends out of state, we had dinner and then played a game. I had never played Mexican Train (a dominoes game) before and ended up playing several games that night. It was a lot of fun.

Remember board games. They are not just for kids. This is a great way for a family or friends to spend time and connect with everyone. Young kids will love the time together and it's a great way for you to connect and have fun with your older kids too.

19 Greeting Cards

Do you spend lots of money on greeting cards and the postage? A cost effective way is to use an online greeting card service. I use one that is less than ten dollars per year and there is no cost for postage. I have set up my contacts in the database with reminders for special dates. I can set the cards up ahead of time or to be sent immediately so nothing slips through the cracks. All at a nominal cost.

20 Goals

What do you want financially from your life? Maybe it's money to pay for your children's college? Maybe it's more money to save for retirement? Maybe it's enough money to be able to live monthly and not worry about how to pay your bills? Whatever you want, today is the day to list what you want here.

---

21 Living Within Your Means

Whatever your goals are, you have to learn to live within your means. That means that you cannot spend more than you earn. For every dollar you bring in, you need to spend less than a dollar so that the remaining amount can be saved.

Go back to the numbers you did earlier this month. Are you including money for savings? If not, you need to figure a way to do that. In a perfect world, you need to have savings for emergencies, savings for retirement and savings for wants. Today, think about how you will get that money to save.

22 Emergency Savings

This is exactly what is says. Emergency savings are for when your car breaks down and you need to repair it because you need it to get to work. It's for when you have an unexpected medical expense that isn't covered by your insurance. Emergency savings are what get you through life, when you are in between jobs. The list goes on and on.

What it's not, is a savings account for your wants. A want is a something you can live without, but you would like to have it. A vacation is a want – you can live without a vacation and still survive. You can live without the latest greatest electronics that come on the market. You get the idea.

Once you have an emergency savings equal to one year (yes, I said one year) of your expenses, then you can move on. Today, plan on how you are going to start to save for emergencies. Set up a regular savings amount from your pay that automatically goes to this account.

If you are saying that you don't have money to save, I will be covering that over the next few months.

23 Retirement Savings

You might be thinking that you don't have enough money to live today, so how can you think about saving for retirement? Yes, that is true. Look at this another way. We are all getting older and retirement will be happening. If you don't start soon, you will have to work the rest of your life.

If you work for a company that offers a 401K or 403B, make sure you take advantage of it. If such a plan is available to you, have you taken advantage of it? If your company offers you matching funds and you haven't taken advantage of this, then you are turning down FREE money. As an added benefit the money you contribute is not taxed now and any growth in your account is not taxed until you withdraw it.

Talk to your company benefits person and start an account as soon as possible. You may need to wait for open enrollment. Have that talk today and mark your calendar for the next open enrollment.

If you already have a retirement savings with your company, up the amount you contribute to increase your account.

24 Retirement Savings

If your company doesn't have a retirement plan, then you should start an IRA or a ROTH IRA. An IRA account is for savings pre-tax money to be able to withdraw later in life when you tax rate should be lower. A ROTH IRA is the opposite. You contribute after tax money now and withdraw tax free at retirement.

Talk with your investment person or tax preparer to determine what is best for you. Discuss the income limits to be able to have these types of accounts and the maximum contribution amounts you can contribute based on your age. Have this discussion today.

25 IRA Accounts

Now that you have determined what type of account is best for you, do your research as to where you want to have this account. Do you want to have this at your bank? Do you want to have this with an investment company? There are many options to choose from and many fees associated with this. Start to research your options.

26 Making Payments for Your Retirement

You now know the type of account(s) that are best for you. You know the best company to do this with. Now you need to determine how you will fund this account.

Do you have the ability to fund the account to the maximum with a onetime payment? One way might be to fund it with your bonus. That might not be possible for everyone. You may need to divide your maximum contribution amount by the number of pay periods per year. This way, you will still be contributing the maximum but with many regular payments. Either way, you need to determine what works for you and set this up.

27 Automatic Payments

Have you ever said to yourself that I will save whatever is left over after I pay my bills? I know that I have. If you are like me, there was no money left over. Big surprise! It's like when you get a raise and you have no idea where the extra money has gone.

The age-old way to save is to set up automatic savings money. Have an amount taken out of your paycheck and deposited directly to your savings account. The money is gone before you get your hands on it. If your company doesn't offer this, that's not a problem. You can have an amount set up to be withdrawn from your checking account on a regular basis. The benefits are that you are saving without effort on your part and the money isn't in your checking account so you can't spend it.

28 Savings Accounts and ATMs

One thing that I have learned over the years is not to have my savings account linked to my debit / ATM card. That way, if I want to make an impulse purchase, I have to put some thought into it and move money either online or at the bank. This delay usually makes me think about the purchase and talk myself out of it.

An added benefit to this is if your card is stolen, the thief cannot access the money in your savings. This is a good thing since most of us keep our money in savings versus checking accounts.

29 Catch Up Day

This has been a jam packed month. The rest of the month should be used to catch up on anything that you haven't completed or something that you need more time to research. One day that you will need more time on is retirement planning. Use this these days and plan the time you need. This is an important step to your financial success.

30 Catch Up Day

Continue to catch up today

31 Catch Up Day

Continue to catch up today

Take Charge of Your Finances in 5 Minutes a Day

Notes — use this space for any follow up to schedule, thoughts and ideas for yourself

April - Organization

You may be thinking what does organization and clutter cleaning have to do with a finances book? My answer is a lot. Are you spending money purchasing something you already own? It can be anything from unorganized kitchen cabinets and buying another spice that is lost amidst the clutter to buying a piece of clothing that you know you have but just can't find because it's tucked in the back of your closet.

April is a time for spring cleaning. The weather is getting better and you feel this energy. A good use of that energy is to start with organization. Start to go through your stuff and put order to your household. Tackle a small project a day. You will love the feeling you get from the sense of accomplishment.

This month is a time to go through your kitchen cabinets, your dresser drawers and closets, the junk drawer we all have. Do you really need all the things you have? Now is the time to sort your things into piles – keep (you need to have a place for these things), toss / recycle, donate / give away and sell.

Figure out what is the easiest and start there. Then work your way up to the big stuff.

I am going to suggest a room or area, but feel free to go out of order. Remember that you will need an area to put things during this process.

1 Stuff Area

You need to decide where you want to have an area for all the stuff you are sorting. Set up an area today for what you want to donate, give away or sell. This area will need space as you are doing your sorting.

2 Start Small

This is not supposed to be a project that overwhelms you. It is supposed to be something quick and easy. Let's start with your kitchen drawers or cabinets. Start with one that is easy and continue from there. Set a timer and start today.

3 Kitchen

Continue with your kitchen today and tomorrow. This is not a detailed organization project. The quick sort is –

> Do you need this item?
> If yes, keep it. If no, determine the next step
> Is it working?
> No, toss or recycle. Yes, is it in working order and can someone else can use it?
> Then put it in the sorting area that you set up.

Not so hard is it?

4 Kitchen

Make sure to organize your food pantry. Place like items together so you will know what you have when you are planning a meal. It makes it easier when you want to write out your shopping list. Buying an extra something when you don't need it is a waste of money. Know what you have and keep it together.

5 Living Room
Now go on to the living room to tackle the stuff. Do you have a pile of magazines that you need to go through? Do you have too many movies or CD's? This is the stuff I am talking about. Start this today.

6 Living Room
Continue with your living room and try to wrap this up today.

7 Moving On
Let's tackle the dining room today. Hopefully, this is a fairly organized area that you use just for dining. If you are using it for some other purpose you may need more organization. Start here.

8 Dining Room
Finish up with the dining room today

9 Bathrooms
Bathrooms can be anything from a powder room with minimal places to store items to large full baths that include linen closets. Toss old products that are past the expiration date. Organize what you are keeping so that you will know what you

need to buy and not be duplicating what you have in your home already. Start to tackle yours today.

10 More Time
Continue on with this bath or a second one.

11 Catch Up Day
I know that this is a lot to do in a short period of time. Keep up the good work and try to wrap up these rooms with two catch up days.

12 Catch Up Day
How are you doing with this? Doesn't an orderly area make you feel good when you see it? I like this feel feeling of order when I enter a room or open a cabinet. I can find what I am looking for quickly without wasting time to search.

13 Bedrooms
What is piling up in your bedroom? Notice I didn't say closet (that's another day). Start with the surfaces and get rid of what you don't absolutely need.

14 Bedroom Drawers
Bedrooms can be a big area. I would suggest that you tackle one drawer a day. If you have kids that are old enough, have them tackle their own room while you do yours.

15 More Drawers
Continue on with the dresser. Have your spouse or significant other do theirs as well. Two people work better than one.

16 More Drawers
I know that you cannot finish your bedroom dresser in three days, but you can get a great start. If you have more time one day than another, spend some extra time to complete this.

17 Bedroom Closet
The bedroom closet – this is not where you close the book and put it on the shelf for later. Do a quick sort with three or four piles. Pile one is the items you know you want and are going back in the closet. Pile two is to get rid of. You don't need to decide now what you are going to do with the items. Pile three is for trying on later. The last pile is for to do's such as items to take to the tailor.

18 Closet Time
Continue with your bedroom closet today.

19 More Closet Time
Try to wrap up the initial sorting of the closet today.

20 Piles 2 and 3

Pile 3 is what you need to try on. Do that today. Move clothing you want to keep back into the closet. Add items you want to get rid of into pile 2.

Move your pile 2 to the sorting area. We'll get to this later.

21 Catch Up Day

How is your home looking? You should be seeing big improvements when walking into a room or when opening a drawer or cabinet. Let's try to wrap up this area today.

22 Storage Area

Where do you keep your stuff? Do you have an attic, basement or garage? Maybe you have all three. Every home is different; you get to tackle your storage area. Pick one to start today.

23 Attic

What do you keep in your attic? Take a good look around today and see what you need to do.

24 Basement

This is my storage area. I have it pretty well organized, but from time to time things seem to accumulate here and it needs a going through. What does yours look like? Start to make a plan for your basement.

25 Garage
Yes, I have one of these too and this is my sorting area. I need to keep on top of this area or I won't be able to put the cars in the garage. What do you need to do to organize this area? Make a plan to get started.

26 Unwanted Stuff
Now you are going to tackle your unwanted stuff. Have you been keeping it in the piles like I suggested? Then you are in great shape. If not, try to get those piles together today, because you are going to tackle a pile a day.

27 Give Away
Do you have specific people in mind for specific items that you want to give away? Great! As you contact these people ask them if they want the item. The next time you see them, bring it with you. It's as simple as that.

28 Donate
Do you have stuff that you don't want that is in good shape and working order? Then check into the charities that are in your community and donate your items.

Remember, if you want a tax receipt for your donation you need to have an itemized list of the items. Check with your tax preparer for your specific requirements.

29 Sell

This is an easy day. Leave these items alone, we will tackle this project in the month of June. You can continue to add to this area.

30 Catch Up Day

You know the deal by now. Finish up what you haven't completed this month.

Now that you have gone through your home and have started this project, you will be amazed at all the things you were able to get rid of. Less stuff means less to clean. I know that when I walk into a room that is clutter free, I have a sense of peace that comes over me. I personally need that feeling after a long stressful day. The calming effect makes all the effort you have put forth to get organized all worthwhile.

Before you go out and buy more stuff, think about do you really need it, do you have a place for it, and can you do without it? If you determine that you need to buy it, can you buy it used or on sale? The first time I did this to my house, I got rid of a tremendous amount of stuff. I had items that I knew family and friends could put to good use – I gave them the item. I made numerous donations to charities, items that were in great condition but I no longer had a need for. I held a tag sale and made several hundred dollars in cash. I sold some items on Craig's List for more cash. Think of all the possibilities.

Thrive In Five

Notes – use this space for any follow up to schedule, thoughts and ideas for yourself

May – Clutter Cleaning

Just like many of you, things seem to accumulate in my home. I really wasn't aware of how this happened until I made a conscious decision to open my eyes. I spent most of last year going through purging and tossing, donating, recycling and selling. I took some time each and every week to tackle a little more.

1 Wallet

Let's start easy and take 5 minutes to look at your wallet. To borrow a phrase from a TV commercial "what's in your wallet?" Go through your wallet and get rid of what you don't need or shouldn't be there. The less you carry the less you will have to replace if you lose your wallet or it gets stolen.

2 Wallet Tips

These items should not be kept in your wallet
- Social Security card
- Anything with your whole social security number on it.
- Any credit cards that you are not using, keep one card in your wallet in case of emergencies.
- Make sure that you don't have your PIN number written in your wallet

Remove these items today.

3 Preparing Your Wallet

Now that you wallet is ready to go, can you tell me exactly everything that is in your wallet? Probably not. So, if you lost your wallet or worse yet someone stole it, you would be in trouble.

The next step is to make two copies of the contents of your wallet. Take the items to a copier and make copies. Remember to remove your items from the copier. One way to remember to do this is for you to write on the copies the telephone number that you would need to call if you lost the item. Now do that.

You ask why two copies? One copy is for you to store in a safe place, like a safety deposit box or home safe. This is not something that you want to leave lying around. We'll deal with the second copy tomorrow.

4 Trusted Person

You made a second copy so that someone can act on your behalf. If you are on vacation and your wallet is stolen, do you think you can remember every item in your wallet? If you can, can you remember the telephone number to call? Probably not.

With my way, all you have to do is contact the person with your copy and ask them to immediately call the numbers that are on your list. Now this is a question that will require serious thought on your part. Who should hold your second copy of your wallet? The person you entrust to this duty could use your information for personal gain. Personally mine is with the executor of my estate.

5 Do NOT Call List

If you are like me, there is never enough time in the day to accomplish all that I want. So, I need to eliminate all the unnecessary distractions. First thing for me was to register all my phone numbers on the Do NOT Call List. You can register your home and cell phones numbers by going to www.DoNotCall.gov. If you don't have an active email, you may call 888-382-1222.

This will stop telemarketing calls about a month after your register. This does NOT stop political, charities, survey calls nor will it stop calls from companies that you have a relationship with. This cuts down the majority of the calls in my house.

6 Junk Mail

Junk mail is a big problem for people. It can lead to identity theft with pre-approved credit card offers getting into the wrong hands and can rob you of your time by having to sort through all the mail your receive.

Register with the Direct Marketing Association www.DMAChoice.org to remove your name from their lists. You can opt out of pre-approved credit card offers by calling 888-567-8688 or www.OptOutPrescreen.com. Catalogue Choice will do the work for you by taking you off catalogue mailings www.CatalogChoice.org.

For a small fee, Green Dime will do the work for you by removing your from catalogues you don't want and they will plant up to 10 trees. www.GreenDimes.org 41 Pounds will contact many direct mail companies to remove your name and part of your fee will go to a non-profit of your choice www.41Pounds.org. Their name comes from the amount of junk mail a person receives in a year.

7 Unwanted Faxes

Do you have a fax at home? If you don't then you get the day off. When I had a fax with a direct line, half the faxes I would receive would be things that I have no interest in and didn't request. I have since switched to an e-fax and the junk faxes have stopped.

If this is a problem for you, there is a solution – The Junk Fax Prevention Act which cut down on faxes sent to homes. You can only receive faxes from businesses that you have an existing relationship with or ones you provided with your fax number.

All faxes are required to be clear on how to opt out of receiving future faxes. Therefore, you can opt out by following the instructions on the unwanted fax. If this doesn't work, you can file a claim with the FCC.

8 Filing System

There will probably never be a paperless society. Life requires us to keep paper be it for a short time, a long time or even for a lifetime. The only way I see this working is to be organized with your paper.

I created my filing system with file folders in hanging folders in a file cabinet.

Hanging Folders such as Auto, Banking, Certificates, Credit Cards, Education, Employment, Estates, Insurance, Investments, Medical, Mortgages, Pets and Tenants.

File Folders go in each hanging folder. For example under Auto, there is a folder for each one of our cars. These folders contain the purchasing paperwork, the repair and maintenance records and any accident paperwork.

For a complete list of my filing system, see Appendix **May 8**

9 Another Filing System

The second filing system is for things – the manuals for an appliance, the receipt for the purchase, the warranty etc. I use a similar set up for important paperwork. In another drawer of the filing cabinet, I created this second filing system.

Hanging Folders for Cell Phones, Computers, Electronics, Garage, Home by Rooms, Outdoors, and Software.

This documentation only needs to be kept for as long as you have the item. For example, the paperwork on your lawnmower should be kept in a file. If you need to refer back to the manual for a question, it's where you can find it. If you have to have a repair and need to prove that you are still in the warranty period, then you have the receipt stapled inside the manual. If you decide to get rid of the lawnmower, you will have the manual to pass on to the next person or to toss if you are getting rid of the machine. Remember to remove the receipt with your personal information before giving the manual away.

10 Your Filing System

Think about how you want to set up your filing system. How do you want to set yours up? Use my way or another way that works for you. What will work best for you? Today is the day to set up your own system. If you need to buy supplies, go do so.

11 Your Files

This is a big project that needs to be tackled. Don't overwhelm yourself by trying to do this in one weekend. I have tried that and it didn't work. I used every excuse to do something else. Start by tackling a pile of papers, set a timer and spend 5 minutes doing this each day for the next five days.

We all have hectic lives and when I come home I want to have a calm feeling when I enter my door. Not a continuation of the hectic busy lifestyle I lead outside my home. For me, one of the best feelings in the world is to walk into my home and know everything is in order. I am not talking about the perfect home that I remember from my grandmother where everything was perfect. This is real life and in real life you can't achieve perfection. Perfection is too stressful for me (I have tried that). Order is what I am going after. There is a difference.

12 Day of Sorting

13 Day of Sorting

14 Day of Sorting

15 Day of Sorting

16 What to do with the other stuff?

If you are like me, there is now a pile of other stuff. Stuff that you are not sure if you should keep, toss or shred.

Here are my rules –
Keep – important papers.
Toss or Recycle – junk mail, political literature,
Shred – I shred anything that has my personal information – signature, social security number, account numbers or passwords / PINs. These include - solicitation offers in the mail, pre approved credit card applications, records that I no longer need to keep etc.

See appendix **May 16** for a detailed list of what to keep and for how long

17 Keep Day

Take those keep papers and start filing in your new filing system. If you get in the habit of filing papers regularly, then you will not have the paper build up and waste your precious time looking for something when you need it. Take time today to file the papers you need to keep.

18 Toss or Recycle

Hopefully when you were sorting you were tossing or recycling the papers as you went along. If not, today is the day to do this. Make sure what you are tossing or recycling doesn't contain your personal information. Take one last look before getting rid of the pile. Rip out your personal information for tomorrow, the shred day.

19 Shredding

If your household is like mine, you have a lot to shred. This can become a full time job. I know that some states offer a free shredding day. Some of my friends accumulate everything they need to shred and take it there on this date. This is a great service, but my state doesn't have this (hopefully soon), so I have to shred papers with personal data myself.

If you don't already have one, get a great shredder. Cross or diamond cut is my personal preference. Put this in a location that is convenient for you to use. That way you will use it often and not create another pile in your life. Today, start your shredding or research when your state has a shredding day.

20 The things in your home

If you are on a clutter cleaning binge, then you may want to tackle the things in your home. Consider each and every item. Do you love it? Do you need it? Does it serve a purpose? There is no reason to keep something that doesn't work for you.

Some areas that I needed to work on in my home besides the general amount of things were my collection of books, movies and music, photos etc. For books, I needed to figure if they were books that I only will read once or a book that I would refer back to. Movies and music was a no brainer for me. With Netflix, I can watch anything that I want to when I want to, so the movies went. With my iPod, I eliminated quite a bit of the physical CDs. Yes, I do have a back up file just in case.

All those actual photos from before the digital era are a problem for me. I needed to find a way to sort and store them. First, I needed to go through them and sort into several piles. The photos I wanted to keep and to sort them by who they were or the subject. This was too big a project for me, so I hired a teenager to scan all the photos and they are now stored on my hard drive. Then there was a box of photos I had no clue who these people or what these places were. That's another whole topic.

This is a project to tackle a little each day or every weekend. One pile or drawer etc at a sitting. If this is too much for you, don't be afraid to hire someone to help or do this for you.

21 Day of Sorting

I am going to give you five days to start this project. I said start. This is not something that was created in a day, so it will take a long time to tackle this problem. The rewards are tremendous.

22 Another Day of Sorting

23 Another Day of Sorting

24 Another Day of Sorting

25 Another Day of Sorting

26 Catch Up Day
This has been a busy month for you and there were only a few catch up days. I am going to give you the rest of this month to complete the things that you need more time to do. Do you need more time for filing? Do you need more time for sorting? Maybe more time to handle that pile of shred? Move forward on any project you need more time for this month. Once you start, you will see how rewarding it can be.

27 Catch Up Day
Even with all my organized files, I am starting to get rid of paper. I have started to scan or in my case fax documents I want to keep and save them to a portable hard drive. The system is similar to my old paper way of storing. I have computer folders that correspond to my paper ones and I have begun to save the documents this way.

One project that I am tackling now is my recipes. I have numerous clippings and recipes handed down from my family that had gotten out of control. This will be a big step towards organization. Once you finish the paperwork in your home, what are you holding on to? My next project will be sorting the numerous family photos and putting them into order.

28 Catch Up Day

29 Catch Up Day

30 Catch Up Day

31 Catch Up Day

How are you doing with your papers? I am sure that you have started clearing your piles and have made great progress. Doesn't that make you feel good? I do want you to continue on with the next chapter. Use you free days or catch up on the weekends with this until it's complete.

Notes – use this space for any follow up that you might need to schedule

June – Selling or Donating

Now that you have completed May's clutter cleaning, you should be thinking what you're going to do with all this stuff. There are many choices such as giving away, donating, selling (this alone can have many options on its own) or tossing. I am a big believer in giving items a second life. Even if I can't use the item and they are in good condition, it could be useful to someone else.

1 Giving Away

Giving away is obvious. Do you know someone who might want that item? When they were in your home did they admire it? It's as simple as contacting them to ask them. Make a list of people you want to contact about specific items.

2 Contact Day

Today is contact day. Call or email them to ask if they are interested in the item. It's that easy. If they want the item, make plans to get them the item.

3 Drop Off Day

Start by getting those items that someone wanted out of your home. Drop them off today or make plans this week in your calendar of when you will do this.

4 Donating

Donating can mean many things to people. The choices are limitless. You can donate items to a local charity for them to sell to get money and you would receive a tax donation. You can donate items to a charity that uses the items themselves. Each and every charitable organization has items they accept and items they don't. Today, look into a charity that is close to you to see what they need. Most have wish lists on their website or at least what types of things they want.

Here are some general examples to get you thinking –
Animal organizations usually want linens.
Schools, Hospitals and Libraries usually want media (books, CD's, movies).
Food Pantries usually want food, toiletries and seasonal clothing.
Check the Resources section in the back for some of the national organization's contact information.

5 Contact Day

What do you need to do to get those donations ready to go? Some organizations have certain times for drop off or pick up. Plan this into your calendar for the next few days.

Make sure to write a detailed list of what you are donating for tax purposes. Today, check with your tax preparer for specific requirements that you will need to do ahead of time in order to make sure you get your tax deduction.

6 Drop Off Day
Take today and tomorrow to drop off your donations to the organization you have chosen.

7 Drop Off Day
Continue with dropping off your donations.

8 Selling
There are many ways you can sell unwanted items. Possibilities include consignment shops, thrift stores, online selling or classified ads, tag sales and auctions. You need to determine first if you want to do all the work and have the time or is it best to delegate to someone else. Today you need to think about your situation.

9 Consignment Shops
For my area of the country, consignment shops will take specific merchandise from you at specific drop off times and then sell the items in their store. They typically do this and take a percentage of the sale price. You need to research the details for what stores in your area sell and their policies.

The one that I use, charges an annual fee (this is minimal). They have certain drop off hours where they go over each item and accept or decline the item. For the accepted items, we jointly come up with a price and the item is for sale. This is the price for the first 30 days and at 31 days the price is reduced. After 60 days, you can either pick up your merchandise or you make a donation to them. Note – some stores will have different timeframes when they reduce prices and by how much so be sure to check on this before you sign any kind of agreement. I receive an itemized accounting on drop off days and monthly thereafter. Not too much effort on my part.

10 Thrift Shops

Thrift shops work similar to consignment shops except you are donating your items. If the thrift shop is a non-profit then you will get a tax receipt for your donation.

Having cleaned out apartments and houses for family members, this has been an invaluable resource for getting rid of items; getting a tax deduction and hopefully letting someone who can't afford to buy new, get a great deal. You have great items that you can no longer use, they are in great condition, but someone else can. I have given eldercare items to the Red Cross Volunteer Closet, Goodwill and local non-profits over the years. It makes me feel good to know that someone else will benefit from my donations.

11 Online Selling

Online selling is similar to your local newspaper classified section of items for sale.

This is an online version that others outside of your area can see. Therefore, you need to be specific about what you will and won't do. For example, for large items you make want to list "must be able to pick up" etc.

I do sell online through Craigslist, but I am careful. I have sold everything from a Tupperware set to a car and all kinds of items in between. I am cautious about what information I provide and about agreeing to when and where to meet. I don't publish a phone number or address and I have a separate email address for my Craigslist transactions.

With that said, Craigslist www.CraigsList.org is a FREE online website that you can list items you want to sell by geographic location and category. Ads run for 7 days and this is an easy thing to do.

I personally haven't used eBay www.eBay.com, but know of many who do and have been successful with this.

12 Classified Ads

These are similar to online selling except this is the newspaper version. You need to do your research to see what costs, if any, are involved. If there is a cost to pay, this may not be the best solution for the low priced items. Some areas have local newspapers (often published weekly) where the rates to place a classified ad are usually lower than the daily newspapers in your area. Don't overlook those as a way to sell your items a bit less expensively.

13 Tag Sales

Tag sales can be both a money maker and a time consumer. If you interested in this way, you need to determine if you have enough items to sell – ones that people will be interested in buying. Then, do you have the time. If you like this way and don't have the time there are other options. You can hire someone to do this for you. There are companies that will take a percentage of the sales to do everything for you. Another option is community tag sales. We have several in our area, where you pay a fee for a space for the day and you bring your stuff to sell in that space. The benefit to this is that with many people doing this you will get more people than your own sale. Determine if a tag sale is for you.

14 More Tag Sale

If this is one of the options you have selected, get out your calendar and pencil in a date you want to have the sale. Then work backwards for your timeline of what to do and by when. A good plan will help you get the most from your sale.

15 Collectibles

If you have been collecting things for years but no longer want them, they may be very much wanted by other collectors. Check out the internet to find collectors groups in your area where you might be able to sell your collection. Or if you don't need or want the money for your collection, consider donating your items to a local museum or some other institution that may want to include your things in their display.

16 Trash or Treasure

This is a book I highly recommend, *Trash or Treasure: Guide To The Best Buyers* by Tony Hyman. I bought this book years ago and it has paid for itself many times over. After cleaning out a family house, I sold a metal toy steam shovel for $500 to one of the collectors listed in the book who drove over three hours to see the toy.

17 Auctions

If you have items that you don't want anymore and they have some value you may want to investigate having a professional auction house include them in an upcoming auction. Items that lend themselves to this kind of sale include antiques, artwork, stamps, jewelry, coins, baseball cards and more. A very rare baseball card just sold for over $250,000 at auction!

If you have items that are less valuable and you don't know exactly how much to sell them for, an online auction website such as eBay can be the way to go. With eBay you can set a minimum amount that you will sell for and hope that lots of people want your item and bid the price up.

18 Sporting Equipment & Children's Items

For your unwanted sporting equipment that are in good condition, there is a store called Play It Again Sam that will take your used sporting equipment in good condition. You can be compensated in cash or credit for items they sell. Contact www.PlayItAgainSam.com for details, locations and what that store is looking for. Each store may have different needs.

There is also a store called Once Upon A Child that resells children's clothing, toys and furniture in the same manner as Play It Again Sam. If you have children's items, check to see if your area has this store.

19 Books, DVD and other media
Do you have unwanted books, DVD's, video games and CD's collecting dust? There is a website called www.Half.com that you can use to get rid of those items.

20 Catch Up Day
What did you decide to do? Take the next three days to do your research on what you want to sell. The sooner you start, the quicker you will see money coming in.

21 Catch Up Day
Continue with your selling

22 Catch Up Day
Continue with your selling

23 Seasonal
Sometimes it's not the right time of year for you to get rid of your stuff. No one is thinking about buying a snow suit in June. You may need to plan ahead on your calendar for other times during the year that is better suited to sell the items you want to get rid of.

24 Catch Up Day
I know that this was more than the five minutes a day tasks. You have the rest of this month to continue on with what you still need to do – more research, more drop offs, etc

25 Catch Up Day

26 Catch Up Day

27 Catch Up Day

28 Catch Up Day

29 Catch Up Day

30 Catch Up Day

Notes – use this space for any follow up to schedule, thoughts and ideas for yourself

July – Credit

Most people don't realize how much their credit history will affect them. You probably realize that what you do with your mortgage, loans and credit cards will be on your credit report. Did you know that your credit report is used by most landlords before they decide to rent to you? Insurance companies (car, home, renter, etc) use your credit score in determining your insurance premium in some states. Some employers will check your credit report before offering you that job you wanted. To establish your utility accounts (electric, telephone, cell phone, gas, oil, etc), they will look at your credit report, to see if you need to have a down payment or a co-signer before opening an account. The list goes on and on.

The bad news is what you did to your finances years ago will stay with you. Things stay on your credit for seven to ten years (sometimes longer). Keep this in mind as you go forward. The good news is that the longer the history and the older an item, the less it will affect your credit score. This chapter will give you some great insight into credit and get you to understand the details of what it says about you.

1 Order Your Credit Report

Today, I want you to order your credit report for FREE from Annual Credit Report. You can do this online and print the report right away, call to order your report or download the form and order it by mail.

www.AnnualCreditReport.com

877-322-8778
P O Box 105281, Atlanta, GA 30348-5281s

Remember this is the only FREE service to get your credit report. Don't be fooled by others offering you free credit reports if you sign up for something that requires you to pay for something else.

If you do this online, be prepared to answer security questions about your credit history. Each credit reporting agency will ask you several questions that you must answer correctly to be able to get the report online. If you think you will not know the details of you credit, then order your report by phone or mail and you will be receiving the report in about two weeks.

You are entitled to one FREE credit report from each of the three credit reporting agencies once every twelve months. I suggest that you only order ONE credit report from one of the credit reporting agencies today. Then in four months, order another credit report from the second credit reporting agency. Then again, in another four months order the third credit reporting agency. This way you are seeing your credit report three times per year at no cost to you. Go to the Appendix for this date and mark your calendars.

2 Your Credit Score

Each person who has credit will have a credit score. If you are establishing credit for the first time, it can take up to a year before you build enough history to have a credit score. Many companies will sell you a credit score, but you want to be careful of what you buy. The lending and credit industries use a FICO score. This score was developed by Fair Isaac and

Company and that is what almost all of the lenders use. So the old saying buyer beware really applies here. Don't waste your money on a credit score that isn't what you need or won't help you.

Your free credit report doesn't come with your credit score. This is something that you will have to purchase from FICO at www.MyFICO.com. FICO credit scores go from the worst in the mid 300's to the best in the mid 800's. If you are planning on making a purchase that will require financing, then it would be a good idea to get your score. If you want to know where you stand or are working on improving your score, then I would order it as well.

3 What It Says About You

Your credit report is a snapshot of your personal finances on that day. This tells potential creditors how you pay your bills, are you responsible with your money, how much you owe, what type of borrower you are and more.

What do you think your report will say about you?

4 How To Read Your Credit Report – TransUnion

Your credit report from TransUnion will start out with your personal information – name, address, previous address, employment information for the last few employers etc.

The next section explains the notations above each payment month. This explains how your payment was made – current (ok), x (unknown), N/A (not applicable) or a number for the number of days a payment was late. Obviously, you want to have current and N/A for no payment due.

Then you get to the actual information of the report, your individual accounts and the details of the account. The account will start with a summary, such as name and contact information for the creditor, your current balance, when the information was updated, the highest amount that you have owed, your credit limit and any amount past due. Then it will go on to tell how you pay the account, the type of account, who is responsible and when the account was opened.

The next section in the individual account is a snapshot of the account. It has two main parts: a late payment summary for a specific amount of time, and then a grid for the individual payments. You can see that a person had a late payment of 30 days and see exactly when that payment occurred. Remember that the older negative information is the less it hurts your credit score. This can go on for several pages depending on the length of your credit history.

Next you will see your credit inquiries, representing who is looking at your report. Inquires for potential credit will lower your credit score, but they will be listed for much longer. The other type of inquiry which doesn't affect your credit score are for review purposes. Creditors that you have an account with are checking up on you.

There is nothing specific to do today; you will have time to look over your report later this month.

5 How To Read Your Credit Report - Experian

All credit reports contain the same type of information – your personal information, your credit accounts and the details of the accounts – but each give you the information in a different format. That's what can make this confusing to read.

With Experian, they start with just your name, a report number and the date you ordered the report. They go right to your credit accounts with all the details. They list your account name, number and status. Then they list the details that include date opened, when the information was reported, type of account and who is responsible, the credit limit and amount owed. Experian credit reports show the balance history by month for open accounts. They continue on to list any notes about the account such as an increase or decrease in your credit limit. This can be many pages long depending on the length of your history.

Then you will see your credit inquires. Similar to TransUnion, there are inquires for potential credit that affect your credit score and the requests from your current creditors who are reviewing your credit history, that do not affect your credit score. Then Experian lists your personal information, followed by your rights.

This is just information for you to understand. If you are following my suggestion to order your credit report three times per year, you will not have this report for four months.

6 How To Read Your Credit Report - EquiFax

And the third credit reporting agency is EquiFax. This report starts off with a summary of your information, giving you the overall look of your credit history. Then it gets to your individual accounts starting with the largest type – mortgages and then going to smaller accounts. The smaller accounts begin with your installment accounts – auto loans and then continue with your revolving account / credit cards. The details of each account are reported in this section.

This is followed by your recent inquires. Next comes your negative information such as collections and public records. Don't panic, it will state that you have no negative information if you don't. Lastly, your personal information will appear and then your rights.

I know that this is a lot of information for you to absorb in five minutes. I am giving you a lot of information that you will benefit from knowing. But you don't need to know it all at once. You have the book, so you can go back to it when you need it.

For this report, you will not need to act on this until eight months from now. Please see the appendix section to mark your calendar appropriately so that you order your credit reports three times per year.

7 What Makes Up Your Credit Score #1

Your FICO (Fair Isaac and Company) credit score is made up of five factors. For today and the following four days I will tell you in detail about one factor.

The first factor is your payment history. This is the largest part of your credit score and represents 35% of your score. This is simple, how you pay your bills reflects on your credit score. Bottom line, pay your bills on time (or early) and don't risk having your credit score lowered by being late.

Set up payment reminders. Pay your bills online and set them up in advance. Do whatever it takes to get the payment there timely, so this will not be an issue for you.

8 What Makes Up Your Credit Score #2

This factor of credit utilization represents 30% of your score, but this is playing a significant role in this economy for many.

How much of your credit is being used? Do you know? Add up what you owe on all your credit cards and then add up all your credit card limits. Divide what you owe into your limits and come up with a percentage. The higher this number the more it negatively affects your credit score. Yes, you need to use your credit to keep good credit, but carrying large balances month to month is not seen as good. My suggestion is to keep this number lower than 25% to keep your score high.

I understand that in recent months before the Credit Card Act went into effect creditors were lowering credit limits in many cases. You need to work on getting your balances paid down.

Set up a plan to put extra money towards paying off your debt. This should be a high priority not only for your credit score, but for you financial well being.

9 What Makes Up Your Credit Score #3

Fifteen percent of your credit score comes from your credit history. If you are just starting to establish your credit history there is not much that you can do with this one. For those of you with established credit, you build your history over time with what you do (or don't do). You are considered much riskier with a new credit card that has only been opened for a few months versus one that you have had for many years. Time builds this factor.

10 What Makes Up Your Credit Score #4

Your credit mix is worth 10% of your credit score. Your credit mix is what types of credit you have, such as unsecured credit (credit cards, student loans etc) versus secured credit (mortgages, car loans etc). Secured credit is when you borrow money and the creditor has something of value that insures the loan in case you don't repay. A mortgage is secured by the home; a car loan is secured by the car. The creditor can take steps to take that secured item for repayment if you do not make the payments. Your credit score wants to see a mix of credit types for this factor.

11 What Makes Up Your Credit Score #5

The last factor is the new inquiries and represents 10% of your credit score. If you are opening new accounts, each creditor will create a new inquiry on your credit report. In turn, your credit score will be lowered each time, for a short time.

When you are shopping at a store and your sales persons asks you if you have an account with them, don't automatically open a new account for the discount. Think first. If you open accounts with every store you shop at, you will have many accounts and many inquiries and a lower credit score, especially when you do this in a short period of time.

If you are in the market to purchase a car or a home and a few months earlier you went shopping and opened several new credit accounts, this could hurt your chances of being approved for the car or home loan. If nothing else, a lower score can give you a higher interest rate on these big loans. Be aware and think about what you do.

Here is an actual money example to show you what a higher credit score will mean to your wallet –

>Car Loan – 4 years for $20,000
>Good Credit: 5.1% interest rate versus Poor Credit: 15.8%.
>Payment will be $103 more per month, $1,236 more per year or $4,944 over the life of the loan.

12 Collection Items

If you have collection items on your credit, then you need to consider this before taking action. A collection item on your credit is something from your past. Are you in a better place and want to deal with this once and for all?

READ THIS – take a moment to think about what is happening in your financial life now and what your plans are for the next several months. Are you going to be making a major purchase with financing? If the answer is yes, then you need to read very carefully.

You might think settling a collection account is a good thing to do. Yes, it is – but only handled in a specific way. Let's say you are going to be purchasing or refinancing your mortgage in a few months. Have a conversation with your mortgage person and attorney and be honest that you have a collection item you need to settle and how best to do this.

When settling your old collection item, you are bringing the item to the current date. As I mentioned earlier, current items hurt your credit score more than older items. If you do this now and then apply for your mortgage you credit score might be too low to get you the best terms. Some mortgage companies will have you pay them at the closing (so that they know the item is settled). This is to your advantage. You credit score is not affected before the mortgage and your collection is settled.

13 Where Do You Want To Be?

Now that you see how much money you can be saving, what are you going to do today to start to improve your credit?

Write you goal here

_____

What is the first step you are going to take today?

---

14 Read Your Report
By now, you should have received your credit report from TransUnion in the mail. Take today to read through your report and make a note for questions or information that you need to research yourself. You may want to refer back to July 3 for tips.

15 What Did You Find
It's reported that three quarters of credit report contain wrong information – from errors of incorrect employer to accounts that are not yours. Serious errors in information could result in a decline of your credit application. Be proactive and check your credit report for errors and misinformation.

16 Catch Up Day
Do you need more time to read through your credit report? Take today to finish up going through your report.

17 Correcting What's Inaccurate
Typically there is something that needs to be corrected on everyone's report.

Let's start with information that is incorrect. Are there accounts that are yours but contain specific information that is wrong? Is there a payment that is reported as late, that you believe is incorrect? Today is the day to get out your information such as proof of payment, bank statement, cancelled check etc. that proves the payment was made timely.

Get out your bill and compare it to the payment. Does it support what the creditor said or is there an error? Keep this information for a future step coming up.

18 Catch Up Day
Do you need additional time to go through your records to find the proof? Take today to do that.

19 Disputing What's Not Yours
Now we'll tackle what's not yours. Do you have accounts listed on your credit report that are not yours? This would assume that you have no idea what the account is – you have never heard of that company, you have never dealt with that bank, etc. First, take a minute to see if the account number matches something that you have with a different name. It's not unusual as banks are bought out for names to change, but your credit card might be slow to catch up. For retail accounts, to have the store you have a credit card with to have it serviced by a bank and the bank name appears on your credit report.

Take today to try to solve the mystery by contacting the individual creditor.

20 Moving On

If you still have unresolved questions on an account that you don't believe is yours, then you need to dispute the information with TransUnion (since that is the report we are working with).

Each credit reporting agency has a procedure for dealing with disputes. Check the back page of your report from TransUnion for the details of how to dispute an item by mail or by phone. You will need to provide your personal information along with your file number. Your file number can be found on the top right of your credit report.

21 Preparing Your Dispute

You need to file your dispute with the appropriate paperwork. This is where your new filing system and organizational skills come into play. Follow TransUnion's instructions and submit your information.

When you submit your dispute to the credit reporting agency, they will forward your claim to the creditor. There are three possible outcomes for your dispute. First choice is that your proof is correct and the creditor will update their records and in turn update your credit report to reflect this newly corrected information. Hurray!

The second option is that the creditor disagrees with you and the information on your credit report stands. Not too much you can do about this.

The third and last option is that there is no response at all. This happens more often than you think. It's my understanding that the credit reporting agency gets to determine what (if anything) will be corrected. Since this is a third party, your information and documentation are crucial for a determination.

Now you can understand why being on top of your finances and having your documentation in order can play a huge role in your finances both now and in the years to come.

Note: You only have 30 days from the date of your credit report to file a dispute. Do this today and tomorrow if needed.

22 Catch Up Day

This chapter was not meant to overwhelm you but to inform you. Catch your breath and take time to recover today, you deserve a day off.

23 Theft

You are probably asking what this has to do with your finances and especially credit. My answer is a lot! I am going to spend the rest of this month talking about things you can do to protect your finances from theft.

Let's start with where you keep you information. By your information, I mean where are your credit cards, extra checks, bank statements, investment account paperwork, social security and medical insurance cards etc. If you say in your home, I want a more specific answer. Most people I speak with say in a drawer. Wrong answer!

Think about all the people that come into your home – the family, friends, housekeeper, babysitter, repairmen – the list goes on. Do you have the time to watch them every second they are in your home? Probably not. If they wanted to, could one of these people snoop around and find your personal information? Are you getting the picture?

Look around your home today to find a secure place to keep your financial records. Do you have a safe? How about a locking file cabinet? Figure out where to keep your valuable information so that it is safe, secure and easily accessible only to you.

24 Trash

What are you tossing out? Shred your information so that others can't retrieve it. Dumpster Divers are people that will look through trash to see what they can find of value. Don't let this be you. Purchase a shredder today.

25 Passwords

How secure are your passwords? Can they be easily guessed? When is the last time you changed them?

Passwords should be something that is not public record, like your mother's maiden name (this is on your birth certificate), not your telephone number, date of birth, etc. Never keep a list of passwords where someone can find them. If you must keep a list, write down a hint and not the actual password.

The most common passwords are numbers in numerical order (123456 or 987654), the actual word "password", abc123, welcome, welcome123 etc. A strong password should contain numbers, both upper and lower case letters and symbols (if allowed) and should mean something to you and only you.

Today change your passwords to more secure ones that are not easy to guess.

26 Computers

Staying along the lines of your password, what computer are you using? I don't recommend that you use a public computer (or anyone else's) for your secured transactions. Never use the computer at your hotel, library etc to check your bank accounts, or view your credit card statements, etc.

These are public computers and you don't know what is installed on that particular computer. There are programs that will allow people to keep track of each and every key stroke you make. Someone could get your passwords without you knowing it.

Think ahead of time for your needs before you leave the house and find you have a need to use another computer besides your own – this includes the office one.

27 Virus Software

New viruses are being developed every day. To hopefully stay one step ahead, make sure you have the latest virus protection software on your computer AND run updates weekly. Virus software is only good if it's current.

If you haven't done this in a while, run an update today. If you don't have updated software, buy the software and install it today.

28 Monitor Your Accounts

Something that I personally do weekly is to monitor my accounts. I go online (from my home computer) and check my accounts, both bank and credit cards. I actually look at the individual transactions to see what is posted. Is there anything that I don't recognize? Get in the habit of this and check even if you haven't used the account. You never know who has.

29 Your Phone

Do you get calls asking for your personal information? NEVER give out your information unless you have initiated the call. You don't know who is calling.

A while back I opened a new bank account and the bank called to ask for my driver's license number. I politely answered that I would be happy to give them this information the next time I stopped by the bank.

They will understand if the call is legitimate. There are products on the market that you can purchase that you control the numbers that appear on someone's caller ID, changes the sound of your voice and more for a really low cost. So don't trust the caller on the line if you don't make the call.

30 Mail

Sounds simple enough, we use the mail all the time for legitimate purposes. But others don't and you have to be aware and take precautions.

- Don't put your outgoing mail (especially bills) in your mailbox for someone to steal. Take it to an actual postal mailbox to mail.
- Don't bring your mail to work to be mailed. Many companies have the mail sitting on the counter for anyone to take. Again, take it to an actual postal mailbox to mail.
- Don't leave you incoming mail in the mail box all day for others to be able to grab. Talk to your Post Office about what you can do (locked mailbox, slot in your door etc). Maybe have your mail sent to a P O Box.
- Look at your mail promptly. Did you get a declined credit offer when you haven't applied for credit? It could be a sign that someone may be attempting to open a credit card in your name.

There are many ways to steal someone's identity, don't make it easy on them.

31 Credit Freeze

A credit freeze is something that you can do so that your credit report cannot be seen by potential creditors. This will prevent anyone (including you) from opening a new account. Therefore, this will limit the amount of exposure in cases of identity theft.

First, you need to determine what you are planning on happening financially in the next year of your life. If you say that you might be buying a car and need financing, purchasing or refinancing your home or anything else that requires you to have a creditor see your credit report, then this is not the time to freeze your credit report. If you are not expecting anything, then you may want to freeze your credit.

A credit freeze is something that you can do with each of the three credit reporting agencies for a fee. No one will be able to give you credit since your credit report cannot be accessed. There is a fee to each of the three credit reporting agencies to do this, and the fees vary by the state you live in.

In addition, there is a fee to unfreeze your credit report to each of the three credit reporting agencies. This is why you don't want a freeze if you are in search of credit. It could be costly to freeze and unfreeze your credit.

Determine if a credit freeze is right for you. Today, get the details and costs for your state.

Notes – use this space for any follow up to schedule thoughts and ideas for yourself

Take Charge of Your Finances in 5 Minutes a Day

August – Debt Reduction

This is a topic that we all need. American's tend to carry debt from the time that we enter college until much later in life. Unfortunately, some never are able to become debt free. Let's break this cycle and learn to live within our means. For some, that means adopting a simpler lifestyle and cutting out the over spending that got them to where they are. For others, this may only be an occasional problem every now and again. I know for me debt can rear its ugly head from time to time and if I am not on top of my finances and practicing good habits, it can get out of control.

1 Goals
Did you set your financial goals back in March? If not (or if you want to revise them), do this today and tomorrow.

2 Goals
Continue to think about and write down your financial goals. Remember that you can't get from where you are now to your goal without knowing where you are going. Take the time to make at least one goal now

_____

_____

_____

3 Clear Picture
Okay, this is the time to face reality. You need to get out all your bills today and make a list of each and every debt that you owe. I want you to list the creditors name, the amount owed, the minimum payment amount and the interest rate. See Appendix for today.

4 Catch Up Day
Do you need an extra day to complete this? Take today.

5 Eye Opening
Did you have an "aha" moment when you saw what you owed in black and white? Most people underestimate what they owe and are shocked that the numbers are so high when they finally take the time to look at all their debt on one piece of paper. Take your time today and think about what you purchased to have the debt you currently have. Can you even remember? Was it worth it?

6 Thinking
I want you to take today to do some thinking. Think about why you overspend. Take a few minutes to close your eyes and ask yourself "why do I overspend?" Then take as much time as you need and write down whatever comes into your mind (don't analyze what you are thinking, just write). You might be surprised at what you wrote. Give the answers some thought over this month. The answers may not make sense to you today but they could in the future, so keep this piece of paper somewhere you can look at it. Understanding why we do things is an important step (maybe the most important) in trying to

break a habit. If we don't address the underlying reasons we do things, chances are that sooner or later we will slip back into the bad habits that we are trying to eliminate. So refer back to your list often and good luck in figuring this out. Answer the question on the Appendix page.

7 Catch Up Day

Continue to think about why you overspend. For me, this was (and still is) something I have to revisit periodically to reign myself in.

8 Making A Choice

Yes, everyone needs a plan. You can't get from point A to point B without a map.

There are two schools of thought out there on paying off your debt. Option 1 is to pay off your debt starting with the smallest balance and working your way towards the bigger debts. In my experience, people who want a sense of accomplishment, who like to see things crossed off as they are completed, do well with this method. Option 2 is to pay off the debt with the highest interest rate and work your way down to the lowest interest rate. This works well for the person who is bothered by seeing their money go out the door.

The choice is yours, but you must make a choice today.

9 Some Things You Need To Know

Some of you may be feeling overwhelmed at this point. I want to make you aware of three things (the second one tomorrow and the third the day after), that you need to know.

If this is too much for you to handle (maybe you have lost your job and can't find another one, maybe your health is an issue), you might be listening to the radio and hearing commercials for companies that will tell you they can settle your debt for pennies on the dollar. There are companies that may be able to do this, but you need to proceed with caution if this is the way you want to go. If you chose to work with one of these companies only with a non-profit company and do your research before going forward. Many people are in worse situations after making a poor choice. In many cases these for-profit debt reduction companies charge an exorbitant fee which they collect in full before they ever begin to pay off your debts. In the meantime the credit card companies are still hounding you for payment and interest charges and late fees continue to accumulate. Be very careful.

10 Second Thing You Need To Know

The second thing you need to know about settling you debt for less than the full amount are the possible tax implications. If you have a debt and you settle it for 60% of the balance, you may be responsible to pay income tax on the 40% you saved. In most cases you will wind up ahead of the game by doing this because you are only paying a percentage of what was forgiven, but you now will owe it to the IRS so make sure you check with your tax preparer before you make a move.

11 Third Thing You Need To Know
Lastly, you need to keep in mind the five factors that make up a FICO credit score (refer back to July if you need a refresher).

Many people want to close their credit cards as they pay them off so as to not get into debt trouble again. Not a good idea. Remember the percentage of what you owe versus the amount of your credit limits? (July 8). If you close the credit card(s), this will be affected and your utilization percentage will go up and therefore lower your credit score. Don't close accounts as you pay them off.

12 Game Plan
Let's start to payoff this debt. Since you have been working on trimming your expenses and generating more money, can you use that money to pay down this debt? If you still don't have the money to pay down this debt, you need to have a plan.

How are you going to get more money? Do you need to cut back more? Do you need to sell more? Write down twenty ways to get more money to pay down this debt. Write down anything that comes into your mind (don't worry that it's not possible). See what your mind is thinking. Write you lis ton the Appendix.

13 Your List
What came up on your list? Did you think you need to generate more income? Do you think you need to spend less? Either way, you need to take action. Start to put your plan in motion. When you get extra money, pay it towards your debt. Don't let it sit in

your pocket. Money will find a way to be spent. Make a payment as soon as you get the money. Yes, you can make multiple credit card payments in one month to pay the balance off faster.

14 Celebrate

This may seem strange for me to be talking about, but trust me. All work and no play really gets to me. I start to feel a lack in my life and then I can cause more trouble with my finances. What I have learned is that you have to celebrate the little steps of accomplishment in your life.

Today since you have made a plan to tackle your debt, you should celebrate. I am not talking about a night on the town that costs your hundred of dollars. This is debt reduction month. What can you do today by yourself or as a family to celebrate?

15 Refinancing

This is a hard question to ask people, but how long do you intend to stay in the home you own? If the answer is a while, then you might want to refinance your mortgage. Look at your current interest rate and determine how much you could save by lowering your interest rate. If you want to save more, consider shortening the length of your mortgage. They do come in 10, 15, 20 and 35 year lengths in addition to the typical thirty years you are used to seeing. The shorter the length, the less money you pay in interest, but keep in mind that your principal payment will be higher.

16 Car Payment
Is your car payment killing your finances? Then consider getting a less expensive car. Do your research and determine if you could sell your car and purchase another one that is less expensive. You need to do the numbers to see what makes sense. If you are a multi car family, you might just sell one car all together.

17 Part Time Employment
I know that your life is hectic and your don't have the time, but you might need to consider getting a part time job for the time being to supplement your income until the debt is paid off.

If you are overwhelmed with debt, then the debt is controlling your life. You want to get to the point of your controlling your life by living within your means.

18 Credit Cards
If your situation involves credit card debt, then you need to STOP using your credit cards and live on what you earn. I know this is hard but you can't keep over spending. Put those credit cards away and out of your reach so you won't be tempted.

19 Lower Rates
Can you lower your credit card interest rate? If you have good credit, you can open a new credit card with a lower interest rate and consolidate your balance(s) on to one card. Remember to check into the fees associated with a transfer since this becomes part of the cost.

20 Lower Rates
If you find that you can't open a new credit card, call your credit card company and discuss your options. Can they offer you better terms? Mention how long you have been a customer and that you have always paid your bills on time. If the first person says no, then ask to speak with a supervisor. This is not scary, they are people too.

21 Savings Account
This is something that you are going to have to think about and make a decision for yourself. If you have extra money in your savings account, you might want to take some of this money to pay down your debt. Financially it doesn't make sense to pay 15% or more in credit card interest when you are only earning 2% on your saving account.

22 Minimum Payments
Did you notice the changes to your credit card bill? Creditors now have to tell you how long it will take you to pay off your credit card balance if you only pay the minimum payment. That is enough to give you the incentive to pay more. Every dollar helps. Put as much extra as you can each and every month to get your balance lower.

You do need to leave money in your savings account for emergencies. Ideally, I want you to have one year's income in your savings for life's what ifs. You never know what your future holds.

23 Eating Out
I feel as if I deserve the treat of eating out. Therefore, it is a struggle for me when I have to decide if this is something I really want to do and can really afford. I have to watch this every time. Are you eating out and spending money that you don't have? This is a trouble spot for a lot of us. See how much you spend in this category and cut back if necessary.

24 Treats
How much do you spend on this? The quick drink because you are thirsty, the snack when you are on the run, etc. All this adds up to a money leak in your budget. Plan ahead and bring food and drinks with you.

25 Last Resort
As a last resort to help reduce your debt, you can stop your retirement contributions for now (not forever). Take that amount and put it towards your debt to get it paid down faster. Note – I didn't say borrow or withdraw from your retirement accounts.

26 Postpone
Postpone is going to be a habit. If you need a new something, can you live without it for a while? What I mean is if that old TV is working fine and you really want a new HDTV, but you can't afford it now – wait longer to buy it. You don't need the latest greatest thing just because it's on the market.

27 Catch Up Day
Now that I have given you suggestions to reduce your debt, take some time to plan what works for you.

28 Catch Up Day
Make some calls and do some research on what you need to look into.

29 Catch Up Day
Continue to make some calls and do the research needed

30 Catch Up Day
Put your plan in motion. Apply for the lower rate credit card

31 A Look Back
Have you gone back to your note page from August 6? Look at it again today. Do more of the answers make sense to you now? Remember to look at it again in a month from now.

Notes – use this space for any follow up to schedule, thoughts and ideas for yourself

September – No Spending Month

I haven't gone mad. I am totally serious. This month is a no spending month. I am not talking about not paying your bills or living without food. I am talking about not buying those wants. That means no eating out or takeout, no shopping for clothing, no buying the latest greatest electronic gadget etc. Can you go a month without spending?

To help you get through the month, I'm going to give you suggestions for FREE things you can do.

1 Day 1
It's not going to be as bad as you are thinking. Have you ever been at home all day and not gone out – see, you had a no spending day. It's that easy. Do it today.

2 Hide The Credit Cards
You got through day 1, so you know that you can do this. Today is a quick thing – take the credit cards out of your wallet and put them in a safe place. You are NOT going to use them this month.

3 Plan A Picnic
The weather is still nice, plan a picnic at your local beach or park. Take the whole family. You can even invite your friends.

Besides the food, plan fun – bring sporting equipment for something to do.

4 Museums / Art Gallery

Some museums offer FREE days. Check out a museum or art gallery that you have wanted to go to and plan a trip on their free day into your schedule this month. What do you have in your community (or surrounding towns) that you can do for free?

5 Libraries

What does your library have to offer? Mine offers many FREE activities from movies, to book talks, to classes on specific subjects or that teach a new skill. Plan one or more dates into your calendar.

6 Volunteer

Instead of always giving your money, many organizations could use your time. Volunteer your time to help others. If you have a skill they need, offer it to them. Or ask them what they need help with.

7 Stay Home

Is there a project you have been meaning to tackle? It could be anything from catching up on your pile of mail to organizing your closet to organizing your photos. Whatever it is, plan the time into your calendar.

8 Board Games and Puzzles

How long has it been since you have played a board game? I enjoy this after a day outside in the fresh air. Playing a game or doing a puzzle in the evening is a great way to relax. If you can take the weird looks consider having your kids, grandkids, nieces or nephews join you. They may even find out they like the games you played at their age.

9 Take A Walk / Hike

Get out in the fresh air. If you have a dog, take the dog with you. It will great for all of you. Get this in before the weather turns to winter.

10 Sporting Event

How long has it been since you went to a sporting event? You are probably thinking how you can do this for free. What about your local high school game? Bring hot chocolate (or your favorite drink) from home along with a chair or blanket. Check your school's schedule.

11 Reconnect With A Friend

How long has it been since you spoke to _____? Pick up the phone and call to catch up. If they are not available, write them a letter to catch up on what you are doing. This doesn't have to wait until the holidays.

12 Your List

Is there something that you have always wanted to accomplish? I have a list of a hundred things I want to do. I have small FREE things, like going to see Broadway On Broadway (free event in New York City in September) as well as things that I need to plan for like travel to Europe, including a Mediterranean cruise. Make your list today. Don't worry about putting things that aren't free on your list; it doesn't cost anything to put them on the list.

Many goal setting workshops tell you to write down your goals or make a vision board of the things that you want. I have both. I have a list that I keep adding things to (regardless of how big they are) and I have a vision board of pictures of things that I want. Make your list today. Write whatever you think of. No one will be seeing this but you.

13 Vision Board

Yesterday you did the list. Maybe you are more of a visual person and want to see the images. Then start to cut out pictures and phrases from magazines, newspapers, photos, or whatever appeals to you. Store them in a big envelope or box until you are ready to glue them to a board.

You may want to do this with the help of your computer and make this your desktop image. I can't tell you how many things have occurred in my life that was on my board.

14 Reading

Is there a book that you have been meaning to read? Check it out of your library today.

If you are a reader, is there a book club your can join? This will introduce you to others you may not know and keep you from procrastinating on your reading. You may even make a new friend.

15 Sleep

Are you constantly running and have little time for sleep. Take a nap!

16 Teleclass or Webinar

Want to learn something new? What to hear something on a topic that interests you? Take a teleclass or a webinar. Many are free to take. All you need is a phone that you can make a long distance call from or an internet connection.

17 Explore a Town / City

Is there a town or city nearby that you have wanted to explore? Check out what they offer for FREE and make a day of it. You can do this with as many towns as you are interested in.

18 Your Interests

If you had a day with nothing to do, what would you spend the day doing? That's what today is. Maybe you want to spend the day in a book store, maybe you want to take time to sort through your cooking recipes, family photos or sport memorabilia. You get the idea, plan to do this.

19 Go To The Park
Go for a walk or hike in a place you have been meaning to explore. A change to your routine is always something good. Make sure you take some beverages and snacks so you aren't tempted to stop on the way home for something to eat.

20 Bike Ride
If you are not a walker or a hiker, how about a bike ride? Explore an area or park by bike. Think of a place what you have been meaning to explore and plan a half day excursion. Again, don't forget to bring some water or energy drink with you and maybe an energy bar or two.

21 Dog Lovers
How about taking the dog with you on a walk? Dog lovers will know what I mean. It's great for all of you.

22 Your Car
Is it time to clean out your car? Are you carrying around too much stuff? Clean out your car of unwanted stuff that shouldn't be in there. Take an inventory of all the items that should be there (and go buy those that you absolutely should have for your safety even though this is a no spending month). Take out the sun screen and replace with the snow scraper. Maybe even vacuum out the interior of the car.

23 Your Car
Now that you have addressed the interior of your car, how about the outside? Does it need a wash? How about doing it yourself with a hose and soap to make the outside as clean as the inside.

24 Movie
Watch a favorite classic movie (or a new one) that you love. Remember FREE movie rental from your library. Make the popcorn and you are all set to go.

25 Play with Kids
Play with your grandkids, nieces and nephews, godchildren and just have fun like a kid. See what they want to do and go for it. We went to our nephew's son's championship football game to watch him play. He was thrilled to have us there and asked us to come back next year. Yes, they did win.

26 Organization
Do you have more sorting to do from April? Take some time to complete that this month.

27 Clutter Cleaning
Do you have more clutter cleaning to do from May? Is there an area you didn't get to? Or maybe the clutter snuck back in to your home? Plan time to do this.

28 Selling / Donating
Maybe there are more items to sell, donate or toss. Plan to catch up on this today.

29 Jump Start
Get a jump start on the upcoming holidays. Plan who you want to spend time with and make plans before everyone is too busy.

30 Last Day
Since this is your last day of the no spending month, what have you learned? Can you live without some things? Are you going to think before you spend your hard earned money? Vow to make changes to the way you live.

Notes – use this space for any follow up to schedule, thoughts and ideas for yourself

October – More Income / Planning Ahead

If there isn't enough stress in your life, it's time to start thinking about the holidays. We all tend to spend more than we had planned and for some that creates the problem in January when you get all the credit card bills. This year I am going to suggest a different plan of attack – generating more money now so that you go into the holidays with less financial stress (I can't do anything about all the other stress associated with this time of the year). Some suggestions are designed to either raise money for the holidays or cut expenses to free up additional cash for the holidays. The other major category of ideas deals with planning for the future by making sure you have your financial ducks in a row by making sure you have several important legal documents in place, so you make your own financial decision and chose what you want (or don't want).

1 Books
Use your FREE options. Take books out of the library instead of purchasing them. How many times do you buy a book and never read it or read it once and be done with it? Save your money and only buy it if you know you will refer to it often.

2 CD's
Use your FREE options. Use the library to borrow CD's instead of purchasing them. People tell me all the time that you cannot get the CD you want when you are there. In my experience, the

library will let you reserve a CD and will notify you that it has arrived. Go online or stop by to find out what your library's policies are to reserve what you want to listen to.

3 DVD's

Use your FREE options. Again, I can't say enough about the public libraries - it can be a tremendous help with your income. Have you borrowed your latest movie in VHS or DVD format? Use this just like you would a rental place, except skip the fees. You can reserve a movie so that when you stop in it isn't a hit or miss.

4 Save Your Cash

Use your FREE options. I probably sound like a broken record about libraries. Ours has FREE movies on Friday nights. They range from old classics to, recent movies and everything in between, such as foreign films, documentaries etc. Personally, I like this so much more than the traditional movie theater.

5 Job Benefits

Have you checked out your company benefits lately? No, I am not talking about your medical benefits. I am talking about the perks that some companies offer their employees. Do they have tickets to sporting events? Do they sponsor a community event? Do they reimburse you for classes? All these things add up.

I know that through the company my husband worked for we have gone to car events at no cost (my husband is a big car enthusiast). We saved $20 admission fee each, because sponsors get tickets. When I was growing up, my father was always given sporting event tickets for the family through his work. Ask and see what your company may offer.

6 Community Events
What does your community offer its residents? Mine offers movies in the park – a night of an outdoor movie that we bring a picnic to and make a night of. We have concerts in the park and at the beach that are FREE to residents. Check out your town and see what is going on.

7 Charity Events
Want to save money, help others and yourself? Then consider the many charity walks and runs. In my area, we have many events that help a variety of charities. You can pick the events or the charities of your choice. You are helping others and getting a great workout for your own health.

8 Trading Your Time
This can be simple as you want it to be. You can trade with a friend – swapping babysitting for each other. I know of a friend who one morning each month, goes to the other person's home and does filing, sorting, shredding or whatever needs to be done for a few hours. Then the next time it is reversed at the other person's home. It's a great way to accomplish something, catch up with a friend and the time goes by quickly. What could you do for someone else?

9 Bartering
Bartering is when you trade an item or service for another. There are many websites that you can research and barter with or you can do this on your own with someone else. I haven't done this personally through a website. But I have traded my skills with others for something they can do for me.

10 Making Extra Money
You could take on a part time job for the holiday season. Companies are hiring now. I did this many years ago to pay down my debt and worked for a major retailer part time. For me, this turned into a part time year round job and I used the money to pay off my debt.

If you find a way to earn an extra $500 per month that is $6,000 a year you can use to fund your goals!

11 Another Idea
Maybe you were thinking yesterday I don't have the time for another job or that you can't leave your kids (the cost of a babysitter would defeat the extra earnings). Here's another idea to earn extra money, what are you good at that you could do at home while the kids are around?

I know a woman who likes to bake. She bakes cakes for birthdays, parties and weddings for others and earns extra money. Do you have knowledge that you think others would be interested in? Turn that knowledge into a class. You can offer it through your continuing education department and be paid to share your expertise. Is there an exercise class that you love to do? Why not find out what is needed for you to teach that class. You will be exercising and earning money at the same time.

12 Consulting / Projects

Can you get a consulting job? You have many skills that companies need. Can you offer your services on a project basis for additional income? Many can be done from your home. Entrepreneurs are always looking for a task to be done on a project basis. What can you offer that others need?

13 Rebates

Make sure that you do this immediately after making the purchase while you still have all the forms and information together.

14 Take A Class

Is there a class that you could take to improve your job skills? Would the completion of the class put you in line for a job promotion? Plan to do this.

15 Off Season

Think off season. Companies that would be slow and looking for work may give you a better price than when they are busy and in high demand. Off season at this time of year would be patio furniture, barbeque grills, summer clothing, etc. Now might be the time to make the purchase and store it until the time when you can use it.

16 Season Specials

Think end or beginning of a season specials. Check out end of season to have your air conditioning checked out. Or pre-season to have your furnace cleaned and serviced before winter arrives. Usually companies will offer before and after season specials (their slow time) for you to take advantage of.

17 Getting Ahead

Are there items you want to purchase that are a big expense? Think about layaway. This is where you purchase an item with a down payment and make regular payments until the item is paid for. This way, you won't be breaking your budget with a big outlay of cash. Nor will you be tempted to run up your credit cards during the holiday crunch. Now is the time to do this.

18 Extra Money

Did you finish selling all your unwanted stuff? If not, put the remaining items for sale on the internet, place an ad or consign the items for extra cash. Start now so that you can get the extra cash before the holidays. Who couldn't use extra cash?

19 Shopping

Reverse what you did yesterday. Looking to purchase items you want for yourself or as gifts, try shopping online or at thrift or consignment shops. You can get many new items at a fraction of the original cost.

20 Planning Ahead

While we are in a month of More Income and Planning Ahead, today would be a good time to begin thinking about your financial future and the documents that you should have in place to make sure things are carried out according to your plans and wishes. Think about this today and over the next few days we'll talk about the specific documents that I think are absolutely necessary for you to make sure you have taken care of regardless of your age.

21 Will

Do you have a will? I know that you don't want to think about dying. Would it upset you if something you wanted someone to have, didn't go to them? A will is document that expresses your wishes – what you want others to have or do. Make a list of what you have and who you want to have it. If this is something you dread doing, you might want to list first, second and third choices of people to get an item. Think about this today and plan time to do this now – don't procrastinate.

22 Living Will

Do you want to decide what happens to you if you should find yourself incapacitated in such a way that you were unable to make decisions about your day-to-day living arrangements or your medical care? Of course you do. Well this is the document that states your wishes should you find yourself in that situation. You tell people (your family and medical staff) what you want and what you don't want to have happen to you if you are unable to make the decision. Don't let your loved ones have to make these hard decisions for you or on your behlf. In many cases there are disagreements between relatives as to what to do or worse yet relatives cannot emotionally deal with the responsibility of having to make such decisions. Another thing that could happen is that the courts will have to make a decision for you (they don't know you at all). You should have this document now.

23 Who Would You Trust?

Who would you trust with your finances if you were unable to make financial decisions for yourself? This is a big decision to make and it requires a lot of thought on your part. If you are married or in a relationship with someone, you are probably going to say the other person. I want you to think beyond that. This person could be your first choice, but you need a second one just in case. If you are traveling together and something happens to the two of you, then you need that other person.

Think long and hard about this, because the person you select has full access to your finances. If they are not reliable and ethical, you could be wiped out. This is what is needed for a financial power of attorney. This could come into play if you are recuperating in the hospital from an accident or are on an extended vacation out of the country. The way to accomplish this is to draw up a Financial Power of Attorney. There is a lot of information on the internet about this topic and you should read more about it and then consult an attorney to draw up the document.

24 Having A Medical Procedure?

You need a healthcare agent or medical power of attorney set up in advance. This is different from a living will since this is to help you now. You could want to have someone with you when you go to the doctors so that you understand everything and can have someone there with you. I was this person for several family members when they were having a planned surgery. Start to think about who you would choose today.

25 Catch Up Day
Use the next few days to continue to think about these legal documents and make some decisions. Do your research.

26 Catch Up Day
Continue to think about these legal documents and make some decisions.

27 Catch Up Day
Find an attorney to have these documents drawn up. If you don't have an attorney, ask your family and friends who they use as their attorney. Ask if they would recommend them to others. Set up an appointment today. Some attorneys will forward you a questionnaire for you to fill in the blanks to create your document.

I don't suggest that you do this on your own with a kit. If your document doesn't have the correct legal wording, the whole document could be invalid. It is worth your money to have the documents done correctly so that your wishes are fulfilled.

28 Catch Up Day

29 Catch Up Day

30 Catch Up Day
Don't make the mistake that so many do. Don't put all this time and effort in to getting your financial life on track and then not execute these documents. You will be required to sign your legal documents with witnesses to complete the process. Make sure you take this last step.

31 A Day Off
I know that this is a tough thing to do for many. I congratulate you for taking this big step. Take the day off knowing that you have earned this.

Notes — use this space for any follow up to schedule, thoughts and ideas for yourself

November – The Holidays

The holidays can be a great time of year for many, but for others it can lead to stress and over spending. Which would you prefer? A little planning can go a long way towards peace of mind. There is that saying that used to be about keeping up with the Joneses. In recent year, it seems to me that people want to pass the Joneses. I don't buy into this and neither should you.

The holidays are a time to create memories with family and friends, not to see who can give the most expensive gift. The most memorable gifts are usually the ones that have some meaning behind them. Think about this before you make your list of people to give to and to think what would be a great, meaningful gift to give them.

1 Planning Ahead

To reduce your stress, start to plan ahead. For me, waiting until the last few weeks would drive me crazy. If you start now, you can spread your spending out over the next two months and not be as overwhelmed. Today set up your game plan. At a minimum, at a high level it should consist of all the things you need to get done in the next two months.

2 Your Gift List

Make your list of the people who you are going to get gifts for. Make sure you include those "extra people" to whom you usually give a holiday gift. These extras might include your hairdresser, your babysitter, housecleaner, mailman, etc. Also don't forget people to who's home you will be invited to and to who you wish to bring a hostess gift. Is it more people than last year or is it less? If it's more pay close attention to tomorrow's task. If it's the same or fewer than last year, you're in good shape but you should still go through tomorrow's task just in case.

3 Your List Continued

Now that you have your list, are there people on it you would like to stop exchanging gifts with? Are you not sure how to do this? Last year I eliminated some people from my list. I didn't want to be uncomfortable near the holidays if they gave me a gift and I didn't have one in return. I spoke with these people ahead of time and told them of my thoughts and offered an alternative suggestion of spending time together or a long phone call. I still wanted to be connected with them. This worked great for me. How about you? Are there people you want to eliminate from your list? Don't be shy about this step, I have a feeling more people want to stop than let on and they will be relieved that you raised the topic for them.

4 Another Idea

Some large families I know do a kind of lottery way of giving. All the family member names go into a hat and each person draws a name. That is the only person they buy a gift for. Depending on the size of your family, the savings can be substantial. This approach might be the solution to cut back your list.

5 Catch Up Days
Take today to catch up and get your plan and list together for a less stressful holiday season.

6 Money
I know that people will cringe if I mention the word budget, so I'll call it a spending plan. Now that you know who you are buying for, you need to plan the money part. How much can you afford to spend in total (notice I didn't say want to spend)?

Next to each person, put the dollar amount of what you would like to spend on their gift. Then, add them all up for the total. If your total is within your limit, great! If not, how will you cut the money? You can reduce everyone's gift by the same percent you are over or you can be a bit more discriminating by only reducing the amount you spend on certain people. Perhaps there are one or two people still on your list with whom you should consider having the "let's not exchange gifts" discussion with. How you cut is up to you. But remember, it is very important to keep to your spending plan.

7 Last Review
After you've had a night to sleep on the decisions you have made so far this month, are you still okay with the results? Does your spending plan work with your list? Be honest here, no one will see this but you. If you are finding a gap between the two or are uncomfortable with how the final list looks to you for whatever reason, then go back and read days 1 to 6 of this month to see what you can do to make this work.

8 People and Money

Are you now ready to start the holiday season? Now think of what you want to give to each person on your list. I'd list a couple of choices for each person in case your number one item can't be found or it winds up costing you more than you thought.

Are still finding a gap between your money and your list? Have you cut your list down as far as you are willing to go? Have you done all that you wanted to do with the October chapter of More Income? If not, take today to see what you can do to generate more income so that you have the money for your list.

If that still doesn't work, for the next several days I am going to suggest some low cost ideas that you can use to reduce your cash outlay and stay within your spending plan. So don't get discouraged if you aren't 100% comfortable with your plan. As we work through the next week or so, there are a lot of great ideas that you can use.

9 Alternative Ideas

I know that planning ahead makes all the difference to my stress level and time constraints. If I spend a weekend day making food gifts, I am ahead of the plan. It can be anything from a couple of different kinds of cookies and breads, to a special meal. Think outside of the box. If you want to do this, I encourage you to block the time on your calendar now, so that you aren't feeling rushed with no time and another thing on your to do list. Remember that items can be made ahead of time and frozen.

10 Crafts

I use this term loosely. I am not a crafter, so this is a basic idea that anyone can do. Some of my most treasured gifts I have received are photos. This is a very low cost gift and the recipient will have it for years. Can you put together a bunch of photos with a theme? How about photos of that person throughout the years? Maybe organizing the family photos to create an album or book?

11 Offer Your Time

Could you offer your time as the gift? It doesn't have to be at the holidays, it could be after. Would parents of a young child want a night out alone? You could offer to babysit for an evening? For a person who doesn't get out much or lives alone, bring over a home cooked meal and have dinner with them. For a family that has an ill family member, you could bring over a few meals that they could just heat up at their convenience and not have to think about what to make for dinner.

12 A Fun Day

Ever want to do something and you just don't make the time? I'm sure you have a family member or friend that you can think of who is the same way. Plan a trip that includes what the other person has always wanted to do and invite that family member or friend. Is there a play or a movie that you know they will like? Maybe visiting a nearby landmark has always been on their bucket list. Buy tickets and reconnect with that person.

13 Get Together / Gathering

I sometimes do a friend's Thanksgiving Dinner. Get a bunch of friends together and have them over the weekend before Thanksgiving for a dinner. I cook the turkey and some sides. Others bring food – sides, desserts, beverages etc. It's a great get together to spend time with the people you care about.

If this seems overwhelming, you can have people over for after dinner dessert or afternoon tea. You pick the occasion that works best for you and have your friends get together.

Tip – if you chose to do a baking day and that day comes before your gathering, make some extra for your day. Dessert solved!

14 Cookie Exchange

I have a friend who each year does a cookie exchange with the neighbors on her block. They all make one cookie recipe and double the recipe. Then they plan a date to get together for drinks (alcoholic or non) and they exchange cookies. All get extra homemade cookies and have fun doing it.

15 Gift Buying

By now you know who you are going to buy gifts for. You have pared down the list to fit your spending plan. Now is when the rubber meets the road and you actually need to start shopping. You should list a few alternatives for each person on your list, making sure the gifts are within your budget. Begin to check the internet, newspaper ads and whatever else you can think of to ensure you get the best price (or at least a very good one). If you can stand the thought of fighting the crowds remember Black

Friday is a time for really great prices or maybe Cyber Monday to shop online.

16 For The Person Who Has Everything
We all have one of these on our list. Each year you struggle to think of what to get them. How about a donation in their name to a charity that they support? They don't end up with something they are not going to use and you are helping others. Make sure you check out www.Give.org to check out the charity to see how your donation will be spent.

17 Project Day
Make it a fun afternoon with friends. Have several people get together to do a project. You could do a holiday card afternoon, where everyone does their holiday cards together so that the project gets done with fun. You could have a gift wrapping party. There are so many things to do for the upcoming holiday season, the project ideas are limitless.

18 Recipe Book
Do you have great memories of the foods your grandmother made? Make a book out of the recipes that have been handed down for generations. This can be a great gift for others in your family.

19 Family History
All families have memories that they tell when they get together. Make short videos of each person telling a story and

compile them into a short movie for generations to enjoy. This is something that you will treasure after those family members are gone.

20 Quilt
Do you have material or clothing that has good memories associated with them? How about making it into a quilt? My husband didn't want to part with tee shirts he had collected from concerts. We had a quilt made of those memories. I personally don't sew, so I was able to find a company online that did this for me.

21 What Are You Getting For Everyone
Did these suggestions help you? Do you know what you are going to give each person on your list? Did you come up with your own ideas? I would love to know what you did, let me know. Email me at Book@JillRussoFoster.com to send me your suggestions.

With stores competing for your business, you become the winner. Check out the sales, coupons and what stores are offering for the items that you need to get. Stores are starting their sales earlier each year trying to get your business. Make a plan and start to shop as your spending plan allows.

22 Catch Up Day
Before the Thanksgiving shopping days arrive, I want you to continue to research the items you want to purchase and start your comparison shopping. Take the next few days to do this so

that you are set if you chose to shop on Black Friday or Cyber Monday. While you're doing your research find out the stores policy if the item you buy goes on sale at a later date and make sure to check out their price matching policy.

23 Are You Ready for Thanksgiving

With all the thinking about and planning for the holiday gift giving, I hope you haven't let planning for Thanksgiving slip by you. Take today to check your plans for the day and take care of what you need to get done.

24 Holiday Update

In today's world families and friends can be scattered all over the place. Each year, I write a letter to let everyone know what's going on, that I am not in touch with as often as I wish. I personally find four photos from the year and put them on the corners of the paper or email so people far away get to see us.

25 Thanksgiving

Take the day off and celebrate with family and friends.

26 Black Friday

Are you a shopper and out at midnight to get those buys? Are you staying away from the crowds? Maybe you are still with family and friends celebrating. Whatever you do today is fine, because you planned for it.

27 Follow Your Plan

Today, follow what you have planned to get your jump start on the holiday season. Or if you're feeling good about what you've accomplished so far, take the day off and just relax.

28 Relax and Write Your Holiday Letter

As you wind down from the Thanksgiving weekend, today is a great time to write your holiday letter.

29 Cyber Monday

Today is supposedly the biggest shopping day on the internet. Are you taking part in it and starting your shopping from your computer? Spend wisely and stick to your spending plan. Try to find websites with free shipping so that won't eat up your budget. You can do it!

30 What Have You Done

How did you do this month? Are you feeling good? Make a promise to stick with your list of whom and what you're giving to people and stick to your spending plan. If you did the work ahead of time and came up with a plan that you can manage, you will be fine.

Notes – use this space for any follow up to schedule, thoughts and ideas for yourself

December – Money Drains

Because this is a busy month for many, this will be a thinking month. I am going to suggest things to you that I feel are money drains. Things that can be a waste of your hard earned money. We all do some of these things, but be aware of all of them and reduce or avoid them whenever possible. Saving a few dollars a day can add up to more money in your savings. Consider eliminating what you don't need.

1 Storage Space

Storage space to me is a waste of money unless it's for a temporary situation. More stuff than you have the room for is usually stuff you don't really need and therefore paying good money to store it is usually money wasted. Get rid of the stuff in storage and save the cost of storage.

2 Extended Warranties

I used to be totally against extended warranties because they usually are a waste of money. Most of them still are. Determine what it will cost and what you will be saving before purchasing one. They are a huge money maker for the store and the company. Do your research before automatically purchasing one.

3 Credit Monitoring

I personally am against credit monitoring fees. If you can and will monitor your accounts regularly, then don't waste your hard earned money on this service. Check your credit report three times per year and your accounts weekly and you are all set. See the July chapter for more information.

4 Bait and Switch Deals
Ever been shopping for an item you need and find it advertised as being on sale? Then when you go to the store it is out of stock but they happily offer you a more expensive item that you can purchase that day. Your mind is thinking just buy it and have it versus getting a rain check and coming back another time. Think very hard before you do this. Make sure the extra you are spending fits your budget and that it is less than the cost of coming back another day.

5 Memberships
Let me be clear here. There is nothing wrong with memberships if you use them; it's just the fact that so many people make purchases and are charged a monthly fee for services they don't use. Cancel your unused memberships or better yet don't make the purchase in the first place. Another thing to watch out for is the automatically renewing of memberships that will charge your credit card and sign you up again whether or not you really want to continue your membership. Review all of your subscriptions to make sure they are not the automatically renewing kind.

6 Magazine Renewals
If you are getting magazine subscriptions, ever notice how early you start to get renewal offers? Companies are asking for your money earlier and earlier. Why give them you money early?

Save your money until it's time to renew. To check on when your subscription actually expires, check the mailing label, it will usually have a date coded on it somewhere. Another thing to keep in mind is that as your subscription gets closer and closer to expiring the offer to re-subscribe usually gets better.

7 Package Bundles

Yes, packaging is cost advantageous to you. But only if you need all of the services offered. Television and phone companies are great at this. You can get several services at a lower price and only have one bill. Do you really need all the products offered? Consider your lifestyle and what you absolutely need before committing to a contract.

8 Bulk Purchases

Bulk purchases are only a bargain if you will use the whole amount. Items that have a limited shelf life are only good if you know you will consume the whole amount before it goes bad. Think about how much you use and only make this purchase if you can use it all up before it goes bad.

9 Full Service Gas

If you can pump your own gas in your state, then make sure you know how to do it. I can save as much as 30¢ per gallon each time I fill up. Many people tell me that they don't know how. Let me tell you it's easy to do. If you don't know how get a friend (or the gas station attendant) to show you how.

10 Credit Card Interest

This is the biggest waste out there – paying interest on your credit cards. A perfect situation would be to never pay a penny in interest charges. But this is the real world and sometimes it cannot be avoided.

If you learn nothing else from this book, get your finances in order and develop good money habits. That includes getting rid of debt and only charging what you can afford to pay off monthly.

11 Brand Names

I used to be a brand loyal person. Times have changed. I do purchase store brands. Most stores have a policy that you can return an item if it's not right. If your store does this you have nothing to lose by trying new products.

I first started with paper goods. Then I have gone on to try food items. Some are great and I continue to purchase them. Others are not so great and I don't purchase them anymore. Try some lower cost store brand products today, you might be surprised.

12 Sale / Coupon Buying

I am a coupon shopper and try to coordinate items I need to what's on sale. I regularly make out great. But there was a time, that I would make the purchase because of the sale and not because of the need. It's not a bargain if you are buying something that you don't need because of a sale or coupon.

Retailers and marketing people are good at making you think you need something. Isn't that the whole premise of Black Friday sales? With a slow economy, sales are starting earlier and earlier to lure you in to make the purchase.

For me, it means not looking at sale flyers every time they come in the mail, newspaper or online. I only look when I have a specific need and am in the market to purchase right away. Otherwise, I will be tempted. Sometimes you have to think about changing your behavior to protect yourself and your money.

13 Impulse Buying

Like most people, I have to consistently guard against making impulse purchases. You know, the things that stores strategically place right by or in the checkout line. Or those things that have big displays complete with marketing materials to get you to believe you just have to have it. So, if the advertising and marketing worlds have conspired to get us to buy things we don't need, how do we overcome them?

There is no easy answer because we have all been conditioned to buy these kind of items for as long as we can remember. Two things that have helped me avoid the temptation are to make a list of what I am going to the store for and to only bring enough cash with me to pay for what I came to buy. Not bringing a credit card or extra cash sure makes it easy to skip the impulse. Go get what you need and come out. If you passed up an item and then you find you really want it, chances are that you will still be able to buy it later.

14 New Versus Used

Does everything you buy need to be new? You can save a lot of money on some purchases if you buy used. Think of all the retailers and websites that sell used items where there is little quality difference between new and used. Children's clothing (where kids outgrow things before they wear them out), and used books, CD's and DVD's are things that come immediately to mind. Another thing to consider buying used is an automobile; we do this most of the time. Especially consider a "certified" used car where the dealer has thoroughly inspected the vehicle and offers a substantial warranty period to cover anything that goes wrong. Make sure you consider these alternatives the next time you go to buy something. I'm sure if you think about it you can come up with many others items that can be purchased used.

15 ATM Fees

These are a total waste of money. Think about your plans ahead of time and be prepared. There is no need to have to go to an ATM that will cost you a fee. Plan ahead for what you will need. If you find you need more money than you have on you, then think about what you want to buy. Do you really need it or could you live without it?

16 Loaning Money To The IRS

Wouldn't you love to get money loaned to you for several months with no interest? If you are always getting a big refund from the IRS when you file your tax return, then this is exactly what you are doing. Have your withholdings adjusted to get a bigger paycheck. Then save the money in your savings account and get interest on your money. Don't make free loans to the government.

17 Convenience Stores / Vending Machines

Convenience stores and vending machines are a part of life. Unfortunately, their prices are usually a lot higher than what things cost at the grocery store. Think about the upcoming day and bring as many things like snacks and drinks from home as you can in order to save money. Even if you have planned well, try to avoid buying extras at the vending machines or convenience stores.

18 Duplicate Spending

Do you run out of the house each morning without time to pack what you need for the day? Are you buying a beverage for the ride that you could have brought from home? This happens to everyone including me, but I try to be aware and plan ahead. That means I have to think about the next day the night before, so my morning isn't as hectic. When I am hectic, I wind up having to make purchases of items that are already in my home.

19 Parking Tickets

Parking tickets are a total waste of money. Carry coins or cash so that you can put money into the meter. Put extra time in the meter just in case you take longer than you anticipated. That way if you run late you will not get a ticket. The cost of an extra hour is much cheaper than the parking ticket.

20 Overdraft Fees

This is a pet peeve of mine. Overdraft fees are a waste of your money and efforts to improve your finances. Knowing where your finances stand at all times will keep you from overdrawing your checking account and incurring this fee.

21 Check Cashing Fees

Most of you won't know what this fee for cashing a check is. It's a service charge to cash your check. This is for people who don't have a bank account and are using a check cashing service to get cash. Even if you live paycheck to paycheck, have a bank account for your checks. Remember to check out credit unions, the small local banks or savings and loans in your area to see where you can get a basic account with no monthly fee. Even if you have to pay a small service charge each month, it probably will be less than what you are paying to get your checks cashed.

22 Pay Day Lenders

Again, some of you may not be familiar with "payday lenders". They prey upon people who typically are living paycheck to paycheck and run short of cash before their next check comes. If you are using such a service, try to avoid it at all costs. The interest rates they charge are extremely high and once you get into the habit of using them, the cycle becomes hard to break. Think about it. Let's say your take home is usually $300. You run short so you borrow $100. When you get paid you repay the $100 plus $10 interest. Now you only have $190 to get through to your next check. So of course you run short again but now you have to borrow $110 to make it. So when you pay back the $110 plus say $11 interest you will now be $121 short. It could easily become a very expensive habit to break. Try everything you can think of to avoid these services.

23 Paying For Free Things

There are so many free things that your state and local government provide you. It can be astonishing. I was speaking with my State Representative the other day and learned that our fire department has a service to clean out water damage to homes for FREE. I couldn't believe my ears.

I have used many services and advice from the state. Recently, I had to do a complicated transaction at my local Motor Vehicle Department. I was pleasantly surprised that with the help in the state government all was set up ahead of time and went smoothly. I was prepared to spend the better part of the day going from line to line. With the state government assistance I was able to do everything I wanted in one line in less than 30 minutes.

This service was FREE. All I had to do was inquire about how to do what I wanted to do and it all was arranged ahead of time. I knew exactly what paperwork I needed to have and who to see. What services does your state offer so that you don't waste your time and money?

24 Reflect

Take the day to make changes in your financial life. What can you do to start to reduce, eliminate or to save your money?

25 Enjoy
Enjoy the holidays with your family and friends.

26 Catch Up Day
Use the rest of the week to catch up on anything you haven't finished yet. Or hopefully you have kept up so you can just enjoy the holiday season.

27 Catch Up Day

28 Catch Up Day

29 Catch Up Day

30 Mindful Spending
If you take one thing away from this chapter, it is to be mindful of your spending. Think before you make a purchase! What did you do differently this year? I would like to know.

31 Looking Back
Do you feel that you are taking charge of your finances? Remember, this is not a onetime thing and you will not be done forever. This is something that you need to work on throughout your life. My suggestion is to start the book over again tomorrow and build upon what you learned this year and

continue to take steps to improve your finances. For right now celebrate what you have learned this year.

Here's wishing you a Happy and Financially Better New Year!

Notes — use this space for any follow up to schedule, thoughts and ideas for yourself

Appendix

March 2 – Knowing Where You Stand

Income

Type of income	Amount received each period	
Salary or wage (after tax)	$	
Salary or wage - second income (after taxes)	$	
Child Support or other payments	$	
Regular income from investments (e.g. interest, dividends or rent)	$	
Pension or Social Security (after taxes)	$	
	$	
TOTAL INCOME	$	

Expenses

Deposits to savings accounts		
401K Savings	$	
Regular savings	$	
Regular investments	$	
	$	
	$	
Total deposits to savings	$	

Education expenses		
Tuition	$	
Books and uniforms	$	
Camps/excursions	$	
	$	
	$	
	$	
Total education expenses	**$**	

Household expenses		
Rent	$	
Condo / Co-Op Fees	$	
Repairs	$	
Gas	$	
Electricity	$	
Water	$	
Telephone/mobile	$	
Internet	$	
Cable/TV	$	
Furniture	$	
Appliances	$	
Groceries	$	
Gardening	$	
Snow Plow	$	
	$	
	$	
	$	
Total household expenses	**$**	

Take Charge of Your Finances in 5 Minutes a Day

Debt repayments	
Mortgage	$
Car loan	$
Credit cards	$
Personal loans	$
Store cards	$
Lay-aways	$
	$
	$
Total debt repayments	$

Transportation expenses	
Car registration	$
Parking	$
Fuel	$
Repairs/maintenance	$
Driver's License	$
	$
Total transportation expenses	$

Personal expenses	
Clothes and shoes	$
Hair and beauty	$
	$
Total personal expenses	$

Medical expenses		
Doctor	$	
Dentist	$	
Prescriptions	$	
	$	
Total medical expenses	$	
Insurance		
Home and contents	$	
Car	$	
Health	$	
Life	$	
	$	
	$	
Total insurance	$	
Other expenses		
Child care	$	
Child support payments	$	
Gifts	$	
Donations	$	
Hobbies and sports	$	
Subscriptions	$	
Newspapers and magazines	$	
Movies and DVDs	$	
Restaurants and takeaway	$	
Alcohol and cigarettes	$	
Pet food	$	
Other pet costs	$	
	$	
	$	

	$
	$
	$
Total other expenses	$

May 8 – Filing System

Here is the detailed list of how I have set up my filing system for all the paperwork that I consider to be important in my life. You will have additional categories that I don't include or you eliminate categories that don't apply to you.

Hanging Folders are in **bold** and then the File Folders under list with each category:

Auto
      Car #1
      Car #2

Bank / Credit Union
I have one folder for each bank / credit union. I do put multiple accounts with the same bank into one folder.
      Bank / Credit Union #1
      Bank / Credit Union #2
      Bank / Credit Union #3

Certificates
This folder holds important certificates, such as birth, marriage, military discharge

Credit Cards

Credit card insurance is something that I purchased many years ago for a lifetime fee. I wouldn't do it anymore, but I continue with it since I did this a long time ago.
    Open Credit Cards
    Closed Credit Cards

Education

Employment
In this folder there are the records for each and every job. From the job description, the offer letter, the benefits information, promotions, resignation letter / termination paperwork. I keep folders for each employer.
    Employer #1
    Employer #2
    Employer #3

Estates

Insurance
This is a big folder in my home, because there are so many different types of insurance coverage that I carry
    Auto
    Credit Card
    Disability
    Home
    Life
    Long Term Care
    Umbrella

Investments
I use one folder for each company that I have an account with

Medical / Dental
I use one folder for each doctor and/or each category of doctor
    Doctor #1
    Doctor #2
    Doctor #3
    Screenings and Tests

Mortgage
I use one folder for each mortgage. So when I refinance, that means another folder.
    Mortgage #1
    Mortgage #2
    Second Mortgage

Pets
I use one folder for each pet. The folder contains the adoption paperwork, all their vet bills and annual shot records and awards.
    Pet #1
    Pet #2

Tenants
I use one folder for each tenant. This folder contacts copies of the rental application, all the disclosures, copy of a rent check, leases etc
    Tenant #1
    Tenant #2
You would only use this category if you own rental property.

May 16 – What To Do With The Other Stuff

Check with your professionals about what they will want you to keep and for how long. As a general rule, I save any paperwork that has to do with taxes, mortgages, home purchases and home improvements.

<u>Bank Receipts</u> – I shred these after I balance the statement and all is fine.

<u>Credit Card Receipts</u> – I shred these after I compare them to the statement and all is fine. Unless the receipt has to do with a purchase of an item that has a warranty or you may need for an insurance claim later or that have to deal with a rebate or a tax deductible expense.

<u>Pay stubs</u> – I keep these until I receive the W-2 and all is in agreement. Then I shred the pay stubs.

July 1 - Order Your Credit Report

Today - Order your credit report today from one of the credit reporting agencies:

Circle that company name –

Trans Union   Experian   EquiFax

November 1 – order your credit report from the second reporting agency

Take Charge of Your Finances in 5 Minutes a Day

Circle that company name –

Trans Union   Experian   EquiFax

March 1 – order your credit report from the second reporting agency
Circle that company name –

Trans Union   Experian   EquiFax

Now you have ordered all three credit reports for FREE and have scene your credit report every four months. Remember to mark your calendar for when to order the next two reports (November and March).

August 3 – Clear Picture

Credit Card Name	Amount Owed	Minimum Payment	Interest Rate

August 6 – Thinking

Take Charge of Your Finances in 5 Minutes a Day

August 12 – Game Plan

1. _____
2. _____
3. _____
4. _____
5. _____
6. _____
7. _____
8. _____
9. _____
10. _____
11. _____
12. _____
13. _____
14. _____
15. _____

16. _____

17. _____

18. _____

19. _____

20. _____

Resources

This book is for information purposes only. It is not meant to be legal, tax and/or financial advice and should NOT be relied upon or treated as legal, tax, and/or financial advice. Please consult your financial and/legal advisors for specific information regarding your personal circumstances.

Recycling Items

There are many options you can do around your home. I personally use a barrel to collect water for the garden and flower beds. I compost some of my waste and leaves. The rest of my trash we carefully consider what to do with it. My town has a great recycling program for newspapers, certain plastics, metal and glass. The trash haulers pick up mixed paper (junk mail, paper and magazines). In addition, I recycle cardboard some other plastics at Whole Foods and cardboard goes to our transfer station in town.

I participate in several town and state special day programs, such as hazardous waste day, prescription / over the counter medication disposal and others. Most of these are located on your states website. I personally am on the email list for our local politician who announces these to his constituents ahead of time.

Costco – has an electronics trade in program at certain times of the year. Check the website for details. You can earn money back in the form of a Costco card.

Target Stores – recycling bins for plastic bags, ink cartridges, glass, plastic, aluminum, cell phones and mp3 players.

Recycle Bank – they recycle a lot of materials through its centers and you are rewarded with coupons.

Whole Foods Market – Number 5 plastics can be dropped off at the stores.

Getting Rid of What You Don't Want

There are many places in each and every community, think locally in addition to these national suggestions.

Automobiles – can be donated www.Auto-Donation.com. Locally, contact your fire department or auto / technical schools; some will take cars for training purposes. In addition, many charities will accept donation of cars for resale.

Blankets, towels and linens – can be donated depending on the condition to local shelters for the homeless, battered women safe homes or to your local humane society.

Books – swap your paperback books with others www.PaperBackSwap.com. Contact used book stores for what they accept. Check with your schools and hospitals to see if they accept books.

Building Materials - Habitat For Humanity ReStore accepts donations of building materials, tools, paint, furniture and appliances to use or resell at the stores. www.Habitat.org/cd/env/restore

Business Attire – Dress for Success accept donations of professional and business attires and accessories to promote economic independence of women. www.DressForSucess.org

Cartridges (Laser and Ink Jet) - Staples accepts toner and ink jet cartridges and will send you money in the form of reward to be used at a store or online.

Cell Phones – can be donated to many programs that will reuse them www.DonateAPhone.com

Clothing – if new or in excellent condition check out your local consignment shop for how they work and what they accept. Check out retro stores for vintage clothing typically more than 20 years old. You can donate clothing to thrift shops and charities.

Coats – donate to a coat drive in the Fall www.OneWarmCoat.org

Computer Equipment - Cristina Foundation collects used computer equipment with an organization that needs it. www.Cristina.org

Dresses – Donate My Dress accept prom and special occasion dresses. www.DoanteMyDress.org

Eyeglasses - Lions Club www.LionsClub.org and One Sight www.OneSight.org accept donations of eyeglasses.

Furniture - Furniture Bank will pick up and distribute your used furniture to families in need. www.FurnitureBank.org. Habitat For Humanity ReStore accepts donations of building materials, tools, paint, furniture and appliances to use or resell at the stores. www.Habitat.org/cd/env/restore

Hangers – wire hangers can be given back to your local dry cleaners

Magazines – can be dropped off at hospitals, nursing homes, veterans' services. Even some doctor's offices and hair salon will take them.

Musical Instruments – can be donated to a schools music program or sell to store Music Go Round www.MusicGoRound.com

Packing Foam or Peanuts – can be dropped off at your local packing and shipping store for them to reuse.

Shoes Material - Nike – Re Use A Shoe Program to recycle your old athletic shoes into other items. For drop off locations and Nike stores www.NikeReUseAShoe.com. Or search for local donation drop off sites by state.

Sporting Equipment - Play It Again, Sports accepts your sports and fitness equipment to them for either cash or trade in for another item. Sports Gift will take your donation of your sporting equipment and will give it to needy children www.SportsGift.org. Second Swing accepts donations www.SecondSwing.com.

Video Games – donate your old video game and they will sell them to fund medical research www.DonateGames.org. To swap or trade your video games check out www.Swap.com and www.Half.com.

Resources

Charities – to research a non-profit organization check out www.Give.org.

Unwanted Mail – to reduce your unwanted mail www.DMAChoice.org, www.OptOutPrescreen.com, www.CatalogueChoice.com, www.GreenDimes.org and www.41Pounds.org.

Unwanted Phone Calls – to register www.DoNotCall.gov or 888-382-1222.

Selling Unwanted Items

Craig's List – online classified ads for jobs, selling items and more by geographic area. www.CraigsList.com

eBay – online auction to sell your items. www.eBay.com

Children's Clothing – www.OnceUponAChild.com.

Sporting Equipment – www.PlayItAgainSam.com.

Savings / Discounts

AAA – Automobile club www.AAA.com.

AARP – An organization that offers discounts with membership to people over 50. www.AARP.org.

Appliances – Check out www.ApplianceRebate.com before you buy an appliance to see if there are rebates available.

Bills – want to save money? Try www.BillShrink.com to see what your options are.

Entertainment Book – a book that you can purchase for your area or an area that you are visiting for discounts and coupons www.Entertainment.com.

Shopping – www.Billeo.com helps you to find the lowest price on the item you want to purchase online.

Vendors

Jacquie Lawson – www.JacquieLawson.com online greeting cards so that you never forget a birthday. Cards available for all occasions.

Websites

Car Fax – www.CarFax.com – you can check to see if a car you are buying is considered a lemon. This is listed under FREE services.

Consumer Action Handbook – www.pueblo.gsa.gov – helps consumers with making purchases and getting help with problems and complaints.

Credit Reports for FREE – www.AnnualCreditReport.com.

Credit Score – www.MyFico.com to get your FICO credit score for a fee.

Do Not Call Registry – www.DoNotCall.gov – to register your telephone numbers and/or file a complaint.

Financial Education – www.MyMoney.gov – by the Financial Literacy and Education Commission provides online financial education resources.

Please go to www.JillRussoFoster.com for an updated resources list as we will be making additions from time to time.

Books

The Complete Tightwad Gazette by Amy Dacyczyn

Clean Your Clutter with Feng Shui by Karen Kingston

How to Organize Just About Everything by Peter Walsh

Not Buying It: My Year Without Shopping by Judith Levine

Trash or Treasure: Guide To The Best Buyers by Tony Hyman

Your Money or Your Life by Vicki Robin and Joe Dominguez

Congratulations!

Now that you have completed the book, you may be wondering what's next or maybe you would like to ask me something.

My passion is to promote personal financial literacy, so that you can make informed choices about what's right for you. I would love to hear from you –

> What you found most helpful in this book?
> Do you have suggestions for improvement?
> What other topics would you like to hear about?

Go to www.JillRussoFoster.com and click on comments.

What's Next?

1. Sign up for my FREE newsletter, *Quick Tips* that will inform you about personal financial topics by going to www.JillRussoFoster.com.

2. Order ***Thrive In Five: Take Charge of Your Finances in 5 Minutes a Day*** for your family and friends. When you order two or more copies, email us a copy of your receipt and you will receive a FREE 15 minute coaching call with Jill. (This is a limited time offer available to the first 250 readers).

3. Attend one of Jill's talks or have her speak to your group. Check out www.JillRussoFoster.com to see her schedule or book a date to have her speak to your group.

We look forward to hearing from you.

www.ingramcontent.com/pod-product-compliance
Lightning Source LLC
Chambersburg PA
CBHW070757100426
42742CB00012B/2169